RAILWAY WORLD ANNUAL

The contrast in railways today is demonstrated by these two photographs of the current railway scene. Above, in Portugal, a 1924-built Henschel narrow-gauge 2-8-2T No E132 is seen with a Sernada de Vouga—Vizeu train on September 7, 1970 and, below, an LMR express hauled by Class 86 No E3106 at Carpenders Park on September 24, 1970. Both these aspects of railways are covered in this edition, with much in between. [A. G. Cattle; J. H. Cooper-Smith

Railway World Annual 1972

Edited by
G. M. KICHENSIDE Associate IRSE

(Editor of the monthly *Railway World*)

LONDON

IAN ALLAN

First published 1971

SBN 7110 0212 6

Published by Ian Allan Ltd, Shepperton, Surrey and printed
in the United Kingdom by A. Wheaton & Co, Exeter

Contents

7 **Interim dieselisation—could BR have done better?** R. A. Barnes
13 **Fifteen to Thirty—and some in between** Photo feature
18 **Flying Scotsman—a Scotsman's pursuit** C. W. R. Bowman
33 **The 2-4-0 portrayed** C. Hamilton Ellis
36 **Weymouth in the last 20 years** S. A. Rocksborough Smith
53 **Something for the workers** R. W. Gwillam
57 **Plymouth to Paddington 20 years ago** W. J. Alcock
65 **Memories of steam** Photo feature
72 **Dirt and leaks in locomotives** W. A. Tuplin
76 **Metroland in 1916** T. B. Peacock
80 **Steam alive on the standard gauge** Photo feature
86 **The Isle of Man Railway, yesterday and today** Photo feature
92 **Alfred Jee—an early engineer** N. R. Webster
96 **The Gysev Railway—an independent international railway**
98 **An electric miscellany** Photo feature
105 **Some aspects of locomotive aesthetics** John A. Lines
111 **Design and its effect on BR stock** Michael Baker
118 **Steam in Germany and Portugal** Photo feature
124 **Corner seat to the Orient** C. Portway

Introduction

THIS YEAR's railway annual under its new title *Railway World Annual* is really the old *Trains Annual* in new guise, much enlarged with more pages and photographs, and allied logically to the popular monthly magazine *Railway World.* It is always difficult to please all tastes but I feel that railway enthusiasts prefer a less studious approach to railways from time to time, which is not always possible in a monthly magazine; in this year's annual I have included one or two articles which, while portraying the railway scene in detail, would have been too lengthy for the limited number of pages in the monthly *Railway World.* The enlarged text space has also allowed the inclusion of what I term fringe articles, which are of railway interest but without railway technicalities. For example Christopher Portway's "Corner seat to the Orient" is more of a travelogue but will be enjoyed by many enthusiasts who wish they had the courage to undertake the same journey.

During the last 3½ years since the end of steam in Britain railways have changed and railway enthusiasts' interests have changed; some enthusiasts actually take an interest in modern forms of traction while others have broadened their interest in steam locomotives by travel abroad to areas where steam is still active in normal everyday service. Again in this year's annual, like its predecessor, the emphasis is still on steam, for I think whatever our interests we are all steam lovers at heart. Not that the modern railway has no place in an annual like this, in fact it does make an appearance, if briefly, in a photo feature devoted to electric traction. I will now sit back and wait for the brickbats and the bouquets (if any). Readers are quick enough to write in when they do not like a particular feature but I should also like to hear from satisfied readers, for their views help in planning future issues.

To those of you for whom this annual is an introduction to railways may I welcome you, and hope also that you will introduce yourselves to the monthly *Railway World*, which has all this and much more on railways old and new. **GMK**

FRONT COVER: The down "Bournemouth Belle" headed by West Country Pacific No 34018 *Axminster* approaches Farnborough in the early 1960s.

West Country Pacific No 34106 *Lydford* storms out of Ilfracombe in May 1964 with the "Atlantic Coast Express". These engines in their rebuilt condition might well have been candidates for oil-firing.
[G. F. Heiron

Interim dieselisation - could BR have done better?

R. A. BARNES

THE MODERNISATION which has been taking place on British Railways has frequently been in stark contrast to the pattern adopted by the Deutsche Bundesbahn (German Federal Railway) especially in the strategy of motive power change. The DB has for some considerable time had a carefully conceived plan of the routes to be electrified and the sequence in which this is to be carried out. British Railways decided on extensive substitution of diesel for steam power in true North American tradition, with minimal electrification. The vast majority of countries in mainland Europe do not appear to agree with this policy of BR and, like Germany, have introduced diesels only on relatively minor lines.

To consider this theme a little more closely a comparison between interim motive power policies of BR (LMR) electrification and the DB Osnabrück–Hamburg electrification is not unreasonable. Both lines link the major centres of population, trade, industry and commerce in their respective countries. In Britain the capital is linked via the second conurbation of Birmingham/Wolverhampton to the industrial, commercial and ocean terminal cities of Liverpool and Manchester. The Osnabrück–Hamburg line is part of the trunk route from Cologne through the Ruhr complex (the region of greatest population and industrial concentration in the German Federal Republic—BRD) to the two busiest sea ports—Bremen and Hamburg, the latter being the largest city at 1.86 million population. The two routes are thus of comparable importance.

Between 1958 and 1962 LMR introduced 104 English Electric type 4 diesel locomotives on the routes being electrified while express steam engines were rapidly withdrawn in response, it would seem, to British Railways' petty prejudice against this form of traction. The schedules of most trains were increased, some drastically, to take into account not only permanent way slowings resulting from the electrification work but also to compensate for the lower maximum power output of the new diesels compared with the steam engines they replaced. In a summary of papers presented before a railway modernisation conference published in June 1961 *Trains Illustrated* (p. 369), the position was summed up:— "It is now realised that a power of 2,000 hp in type 4, being closely equivalent to a class 7 steam power, does not quite meet the most onerous requirements of heavy, fast trains formerly worked by steam class 8, and that locomotives (diesel) having 2,500 to 2,700 hp available *for traction* are also required." The original purpose of these diesels ended in 1966 with the inauguration of the electric service. The London Midland Region then had 100 expensive diesels on its hands of a type which, by then, had been considerably improved in later designs (with a power/

BELOW: Another candidate for conversion to modern forms of steam working would have been the Britannia Pacific, of which class No 70023 *Venus* leaves Bath with the "Bristolian" in the late 1950s. [G. F. Heiron

weight ratio of 15 hp/ton one would hope so!) and the life of some of Britain's best Pacifics was cut tragically short. BR had, I submit, put itself, yet again, further in the red than it need have been.

At this point it is relevant to consider certain points contained in a letter from Mr G. A. Davidson published in full in Mr C. J. Allen's column of October 1963 *Modern Railways* (p. 255). Mr Davidson carefully argues in favour of a fleet of modern steam locomotives in place of dieselisation to operate the fastest possible service, as economically as possible, if BR's limited electrification policy is to be pursued. In his analysis of the letter Mr Allen points out that the 1939 tests on LMS Pacific, *Duchess of Abercorn*, when a maximum drawbar horse-power of 2,511 was recorded, required a ton of coal every 33 miles (or every half-hour) to be shovelled into the firebox. Quite correctly Mr Allen comments "What fireman is likely to be able to stand up regularly to such a strain as that, or, still more, to be prepared to do so?" Later Mr Allen remarks, when discussing why steam traction was not perpetuated. "One of the most urgent matters was the acute difficulty of recruiting young staff for cleaning and firing steam locomotives. . . . ." "Does he (Mr Davidson) propose young men should be press-ganged into the service in order that the dirty work of cleaning and the hot and labourious work of firing, harder than ever before, should continue at existing rates of pay?" This rather facetious comment indicates that Mr Allen did not give due consideration to Mr Davidson's arguments in favour of mechanical or oil firing, the latter Mr Allen briefly dismissed in commenting " . . . . while this (oil firing) might have made possible cleaner operation, and so might have helped slightly in solving the acute problem of recruiting labour for steam locomotive manning and maintenance, it is common knowledge that the burning of oil in a locomotive firebox is about the most thermally inefficient way oil can be used for traction purposes." Mr Allen goes on to indicate his disbelief in Mr Davidson's assertions that oil- or mechanically-fired British Pacifics could generate continuously a

BELOW: A class which was subject to some experiment to improve its efficiency was the BR standard class 9 2-10-0, some of which were fitted with Giesl ejectors, and others, like No 92029, seen here with a west to north excursion at Westerleigh Junction in June 1962, were fitted with Crosti boilers. [G. F. Heiron

drawbar horse-power similar to that of a 2,700 bhp *engined* diesel locomotive. Mr Allen's comments on this occasion are somewhat more myopic than usual and certainly need refuting in the light of German experience. On the point of cost Mr Allen is certainly correct in his remarks of the thermal inefficiency of oil combustion in a steam locomotive firebox, but surely he must be aware of the other savings involved. In the late 1950's conversion to oil-firing was costing the DB approximately 50,000 DM (about £5,000) per locomotive. This capital investment and the greater thermal inefficiency due to oil burning was offset by the savings set out below so that the overall operating costs of the service fell by 20–25 per cent.

1. Lower and falling costs of fuel oil per calorific unit, compared with the spiralling cost of good steam coal;
2. Reduction in the number of staff required for cleaning, fire lighting and disposal;
3. Elimination of capital and maintenance costs on ash disposal and coaling plant. (Provision of oil fuelling equipment is very much cheaper);
4. No fuel wastage in lighting up—10–15 cwt for coal fired engines;
5. Considerable increase in locomotive (and, hence, crew) utilisation. The number of engines and men required to operate a given service thus fell significantly.

This latter factor is one of the most important in the macro-economics of railway operation. The superiority of oil-fired engines over their coal-fired counterparts and their equality to internal combustion engined locomotives in this respect became visually evident to me when visiting Osnabrück motive power depot in north Germany. At 19.00 a fireman signed on for duty and was soon lighting up his 01^{10} Pacific 01 1073. This was a simple matter of soaking a handful of cotton waste in Kerosine, igniting it and then throwing the burning bundle into the firebox with the oil jets on. After adjusting the burners, the fireman proceeded to carry out routine preparation work and was joined by his driver at 19.15. Lubrication and general inspection of the locomotive was concluded by 19.25 whence the locomotive gently receded tender first towards the station which lies about one mile away to the south west. At 19.45 01 1073 passed the depot on the main line to Hamburg with train D595, the 19.42 from Osnabrück Hbf which amounted to eleven coaches or about 440 tons gross—only 40 min after being lit up! Although it is extremely unlikely that this was a completely cold start, this was a highly creditable performance and certainly approximates to the time taken by British Railways diesels.

Proceeding further with the question of locomotive utilisation (not merely availability) which is fundamental to the minimisation of costs on all railway systems, it is of interest to note that the intensive express passenger service between Osnabrück and Hamburg, with the exception of one or two lightweight Fernschnellzug (long distance expresses), was worked entirely by eleven 01^{10} Pacifics based at Osnabrück with certain diagrams covered by Hamburg (Altona) engines or 01 (two-cylinder coal burners) Pacifics based at Bremen, until the electric service began in the autumn of 1968. Steam locomotive utilisation over this route was so good even in its last year that in their annual report of locomotive performances published in *Die Bundesbahn*, December 1968 page 887, the DB says that the 11 oil-fired 01^{10} Pacifics stationed at Osnabrück were *averaging* 883 km (about 547½ miles) per day. At this point a useful comparison can be made with the main line diesel units operating from Altona depot, for although their rosters inevitably involve many more miles on other routes, the services they operate are comparable with those worked by the 01^{10} locomotives. G. Freeman Allen, in his article on page 386 of June 1963 *Modern Railways*, exhalting the virtues of German diesel hydraulics was apparently exceedingly impressed by the fact that the 23 V200's based at Altona achieved a daily average mileage "as high as 569 miles" and this required each engine to spend 16–17 hours per day *in traffic*. This provides a reference by which the achievements of the oil-fired Pacifics can be acclaimed and the performance of EE Type 4's criticised. The report on BR dieselisation (1961), to which I have already referred, notes that daily mileages (*not* average) of English Electric type 4's on London Midland Region lines was no better than 350 (and in the case of BR Sulzer type 4's only 230).

At this juncture it is pertinent to enquire into the capability of oil-fired steam locomotives to work trains diagrammed for EE type 4 haulage or, in fact, if pre-electrification engineering schedules and loads could have been dealt with by such engines when the Western Lines were receiving their face-lift. The question of recruiting staff, as raised by Mr Allen, can be briefly dismissed by pointing out that numerous inquisitions of German drivers having experience of all four forms of traction revealed that the preference of any one driver was invariably; 1-electric, 2-oil-fired steam, 3-diesel, 4-coal-fired steam. Since BR does not seem to be crippled by a shortage of diesel locomen one cannot envisage, on this basis, a shortage of staff for working oil-fired steam locomotives.

The next important matter is that of performance. The limit on continuous power output of a hand-fired steam engine—which has a front end limit above the maximum continuous capacity of the fireman to shovel coal into the firebox—is the fireman (crudely, the locomotive being worked hard could burn more coal than the fireman could supply; a good fireman should just be capable of out-firing a class 4 engine being worked at full power). However, the maximum continuous capacity of an oil-fired steam locomotive, assuming a hypothetical infinite front-end limit, is the maximum continuous steaming rate of the boiler. The 01^{10} Pacifics have dimensions similar to those of the largest British Pacifics. They are no longer than LMS Coronations, having three cylinders 19.7 in. by 24.4 in, driving wheels 6 ft 8 in in diameter, a boiler pressure of 16 kg/sq cm (227.5 lb/sq in) and a grate area (not relevant to oil fired engines) of 46.5 sq ft. Tractive effort is 37,200 lb with 61.14 tons adhesive weight out of the 113.76 tons total.

The maximum continuous steaming rate of the boiler is 33,600 lb/hr, yet a Coronation has been shown capable of producing 40,000 lb/hr continuously with two firemen. The 01^{10} Pacifics will sustain a maximum continuous drawbar horse-power of 1,765 at 30 mph and the Coronations, 2,200 with two firemen at the same speed. On the road such a figure will produce results significantly superior to that of a diesel of greater nominal engine horse power. This is due to internal power losses in the diesel unit which, using the figures of "an Eastern Region Engineer" writing in March 1962 *Modern Railways* (p.174), works out at slightly over 23 per cent for a Brush type 2 locomotive with a 1,255 bhp engine. In addition there are other inherent advantageous characteristics of the reciprocating steam engine's power curve. This latter point is

RIGHT: Steam locomotive servicing in Germany has been helped considerably by improved equipment at depots; this locomotive at Hamburg Altona is having its tubes cleaned with vacuum equipment. [G. Tatton-Brown

expanded by the Engineer thus: ". . . . the steam locomotive can exert a higher tractive effort than a diesel when working at intermittent steam rate; hence, whilst the diesel is better able to work heavy freight trains, the steam locomotive may have an advantage on high speed passenger work if the fireman is able to produce the necessary steam". The potential of an oil fired Coronation Pacific on the Euston–Crewe main line can be assessed from the theoretical calculated timings of "45671" published on page 291 of May 1961 *Trains Illustrated.* A class 7MT locomotive working at 22,000 lb/hr would run the 158 miles from Euston to Crewe in 146 min with a train of 405 tons, assuming a clear road.

Converting British steam locomotives, except the Bulleid Pacifics, to oil firing would have undoubtedly encountered the technical problem of combusting oil in a copper firebox. One wonders, however, if, with the present inflated scrap value of copper, it might even have been economically advantageous to replace copper fireboxes with suitably designed steel ones.

Although I have confined myself in this article to the advantages in converting steam locomotives to oil burning instead of purchasing diesel locomotives as an interim traction form before electrification, the oil-fired reciprocating steam engine has considerable potential as a permanent form of motive power for the future. Recent developments in heating plant technology have made it possible to produce, by extending present techniques slightly, an automatically oil fired locomotive. Such a machine would require only a driver and having all the advantages of a diesel locomotive (and a few more besides) but none of its disadvantages, especially expensive maintenance and large capital investment, it would immediately be considerably cheaper, overall, to operate. The introduction of oil burning compound engines could well produce a motive power revolution of the first magnitude.

BELOW: Oil-fired Class 41 2-8-2 of the German Federal Railway; this one is seen at Vehrte with a car-carrier train in December 1966. [H. Steeneken

Fifteen to thirty —and some in between

RIGHT: Vale of Rheidol 2-6-2T No 7 leaves Aberystwyth for Devils Bridge on September 15, 1970.
[John H. Bird

BELOW: Sister engine No 8 accelerates along the level section of the 1 ft $11\frac{1}{2}$ in gauge of the VoR from Aberystwyth before starting the climb to Devils Bridge with the 14.45 train in August 1970. [J. Reeves

FIFTEEN TO THIRTY

continued

LEFT: Festiniog Railway Fairlie 0-4-4-0T *Earl of Merioneth* leaves Portmadoc and crosses The Cob with a train for Dduallt on September 1, 1969. [G. J. Warrilow

LEFT LOWER: 2 ft 6 in gauge Welshpool and Llanfair 0-6-0T No. 1 *The Earl* crosses Brynelin Viaduct with a train to Castle Caereinion on October 6, 1968. [Allan Stewart

RIGHT: The smallest gauge represented in this feature, the 15 in gauge Romney, Hythe and Dymchurch line; No 2 *Northern Chief* accelerates away from New Romney with a train for Hythe on August 20, 1969. [R. E. B. Siviter

BELOW: Same gauge but at the opposite end of the country; Ravenglass & Eskdale 2-8-2 No 9 *River Mite* approaches Muncaster Mill with the 13.55 Dalegarth—Ravenglass on August 3, 1970. [A. W. Hobson

No 4

ABOVE: Talyllyn Railway No 3 *Sir Haydn,* representing the 2 ft 3 in gauge, stands at Towyn waiting to leave with a train for Abergynolwyn on July 19, 1970. [G. R. Hounsell

LEFT UPPER: Britain's only rack and pinion railway, the Snowdon Mountain Railway, seen in silhouette with a train descending from the summit to Llanberis on August 29, 1970. [P. R. Foster

LEFT: Another Talyllyn train, this time with No 4 *Edward Thomas* approaching Brynglas hauling a mixed collection of coaches on the 15.15 Towyn—Abergynolwyn on July 29, 1970. [G. F. Gillham

ABOVE: Privately-preserved LNER Class A3 Pacific No 4472 *Flying Scotsman* climbs Holloway Bank on September 21, 1968 with the LCGB "East Riding Limited" excursion. [B. A. Reeves

Flying Scotsman - a Scotsman's pursuit

C. W. R. BOWMAN

I CANNOT RECALL exactly when I saw my first A3 Pacific of the erstwhile London & North Eastern Railway, but it would probably be around 1930. We spent many hours "watching trains"—we weren't called locospotters then—at Waverley and other Edinburgh vantage points in the 1930s, and of course, A3s were well to the fore along with the unrebuilt A1s and the brand new A4s. Up to the end of 1953 when I came to live in Canada I had seen about 50 of the A3s. It seems a shocking waste now, but I did not photograph a single one of them. Film was not too plentiful and money even less so. My camera was a pre-1920 Kodak Autographic with a f-11 lens and a *fastest* shutter speed of $\frac{1}{50}$ sec but even so I could have taken standing shots.

Between 1958 and 1962, I returned to Scotland for several visits and saw A3s once more. Particularly do I remember 1961 when Haymarket kept 60043 and 60101 so immaculate for working the "Queen of Scots". And when an announcement appeared in the *Weekly Scotsman* in 1962 about the Gresley A3 Preservation Society, I joined. The target was No 60103 (at that time) *Flying Scotsman* and the aim was to raise the necessary £3,000 to permit purchase from British Rail on withdrawal. When the day of reckoning arrived the Society had not accumulated the required sum and although somewhat disappointed that the Society was not able to purchase the engine, I was very happy that it had in fact been saved from the scrapyard by Alan Pegler. Flying Scotsman was one A3 I had never seen, probably because it was a King's Cross engine, although it must have worked through to Edinburgh many times.

I had been back to Scotland for several holidays, but family matters had prevented me from getting to England until 1963. However, in that year I booked on a charter flight leaving Toronto on June 12. With the dates for the trip arranged well in advance, I was delighted to find out that *Flying Scotsman* was to visit London on June 15. So I was at Marylebone in ample time to have my first-ever sight of 4472 as 'he' arrived from Sheffield with the RPS Great Central Railway Special. My tape recorder was disappointed that the familiar Gresley rod clank was just a whisper of its former self but the sight of an apple-green Pacific, for the first time in about 15 years, was a real joy. My camera duly recorded the engine in colour, first entering the station and then surrounded by the vast crowd of enthusiasts, and I was also able to obtain a few shots without bodies dominating the scene while *Flying Scotsman* stood at the platform end waiting for signals before proceeding to Cricklewood shed for servicing. So began what has become an annual meeting with *Flying Scotsman.*

At the risk of horrifying some die-hard LNER enthusiasts, I must say that, although LNER engines are my first love, I do not dislike Merchant Navy Pacifics, Castles and Black Fives! Before 1964 was very old, I was therefore booked on the company's annual Spring Charter to Britain, arriving London on April 25 and returning to Canada on May 17, to see more BR steam. By coincidence once again, 4472 was in action during my visit, this time in Scotland. The engine's trip North was two-fold. Terence Cuneo was to do one of his outstanding paintings of *Flying Scotsman* on the Forth Bridge and for this purpose 4472 was booked to work a special from Edinburgh to Inverkeithing and back on 11, 12, 13 and 14 May with some standing time allowed on the bridge. Inverkeithing is, of course, two miles north of the bridge and has a triangle which makes it a suitable turning point. On Saturday, May 16, 1964, there was to be an Edinburgh-Aberdeen excursion sponsored by the St. Andrew's University, Queen's College, Dundee Railway and Transport Society, North via Perth and the Caledonian line through Forfar and returning South by way of Montrose, Dundee and Cupar. Little did I know on reading the announcement in the March 1964 issue of *Modern Railways* that there was going to be so much frustration.

On arrival in Edinburgh, I visited my old haunts at St. Margaret's and found that 4472 was to be stabled at Dalry Road—a great honour for another ex-LMS shed!—during her stay in the Scottish capital. I made arrangements to be on shed when the engine arrived from the South on May 9. Although we had no sunshine, the weather was reasonable and I obtained a good series of black-and-white pictures. Here was another first for me —*Flying Scotsman* in Scotland.

To the everlasting credit of Dalry Road MPD, a single-road shed was cleared of its usual diesel occupants to provide a secure stable for the Pacific. The only other occupant of this shed during *Flying Scotsman's* visit was a Caledonian 0-4-4T awaiting preservation, which I believe was BR No 55189.

I found that the best way for me to meet other commitments in the land of the oatmeal savages and still see more of 4472, was to leave Edinburgh on May 10 and return to the area on Thursday, May 14, for the last of the Forth Bridge runs and then team up with my very good friend from Edinburgh, John Murdoch, for the Saturday excursion. My choice of location for the Thursday run was the 1 in 70 climb from Inverkeithing; I was in position well ahead of the booked time. Some two hours later I was beginning to get concerned that 4472 had not appeared and finally concluded that there must have been some change in plans. And so it was. I called in at Dalmeny signalbox on the way in to Edinburgh and found that Terence Cuneo had completed his work on location on the Wednesday and hence the Thursday trip had been understandably cancelled.

Saturday, May 16, dawned overcast and remained that way all day. It was reasonably bright, though, as John and I headed North from Perth to our viewpoint, on the 1 in 125 climb to Stanley Junction. It was here that I was taught a lesson that I shall never forget. The location was a shallow grassy cutting and I was shooting from the top of the bank on the up side so that the steam would show up against the grass. 4472 would be on the down line. We were so full of anticipation that it did not occur to us to check times of up trains at that point. It was a bit windy and to ensure a good recording we had parked the car a short distance down a farm road with the open windows on the lee side and the microphone positioned on the back of the front seat. All set. Then we saw steam about two miles away and we stood enthralled as the glorious three-cylinder chant galloped up the bank towards us, cameras ready. With 4472 a matter of 200 yd away, there was a horrible growl behind us and an English Electric Type 4 trailing nine bogies hurtled by on an up passenger. The two engines passed right opposite the tape recorder, but fortunately the last coach of the up train just got out of the way in time to enable me to obtain one colour shot of *Flying Scotsman*. John was so stunned that he didn't even press his shutter release. The tape recording was spoiled and what was even more galling was the fact that not a single up train passed that point for about ½ hr before and after *Flying Scotsman*. Never were harsher words applied to an English Electric Type 4 in particular and diesels in general.

Still fuming we returned to Perth for lunch and then drove over to Montrose to spend the afternoon at Kinnaber Junction. We felt a bit better after seeing *Silver King* on the up Postal. On the return run, 4472 was booked to follow the 17.15 Aberdeen to Glasgow three-hour express as far as Kinnaber Junction at which point the "Granite City" would take the Caley and *Flying Scotsman* the ex-NBR line to Montrose. The times at Kinnaber were less than 15 min apart. We wanted to get 4472 on the climb out of Montrose, but were reluctant to forego pictures of an A4 on the "Granite City". As soon as *Merlin* had streaked through the junction we made a dash for the car and stormed South. We had little time to spare because we had to go right through the town, although we knew the train would have to slow at Montrose South to collect the single-line tablet and again at Usan to hand it in. As Usan box hove into site, John, acting as observer, saw a plume of steam coming up the bank. However we managed to get into position at the first overbridge South of Usan, where the gradient is 1 in 111, just as 4472 accelerated away from the box at 18.23. The recording was just great, and I have never heard an A3, or any other engine, sound so magnificent as *Flying Scotsman* did on that calm Angus evening. We also got pictures.

It will be recalled that this was on May 16 and my return flight to Canada (from London) was on the following day. The only way I could get to London in time was on the "Night Scotsman" on May 16. As the down "St Mungo" usually produced an A4, we decided that we had just time to see this, and 60009 duly appeared with the 17.30 Glasgow–Aberdeen. It was nearly 20.00 when we left Kinnaber. To reach Edinburgh in time meant some fairly speedy motoring and the car was a Mini, so this meant flat out. There was a slight delay at Perth where a Jaguar with a blue light on top came alongside and wished to engage in conversation. The constable alleged that I had been doing 50 mph in a 30 mph limit and that they had reached 75 trying to catch up through the city. I said I didn't think it had been quite so fast, showed my Canadian licence and said that I had a train to catch. I was let off but warned very forcibly that if they found me doing it again I'd be put behind bars! I made Waverley with 15 min to spare.

In 1965, a rather reverse situation applied. I had to rush right from my London arrival to Edinburgh and drive to the Carlisle area. There was no flight to Carlisle and unfortunately no train connection would have got me to Carlisle in time. It was 10.22 GMT+1 on May 15 when my Air Canada DC-8 touched down at Heathrow. At 12.40 I was off to Edinburgh on a BEA Vanguard and reached Turnhouse at 13.55. John Murdoch met me and without delay we headed for Carlisle 95 miles away, reached in slightly less than two hours as I recall. We did not know the Ais Gill line well and consequently needed time to scout viewpoints. For the first time I was using colour cine film in addition to stills and tape recording. We did not go farther south than Armathwaite, eventually settling on Low House Crossing as the photography and recording point.

Flying Scotsman was booked to haul a Gainsborough Model Railway Society excursion from Lincoln to Dumfries as far as

BELOW: *Flying Scotsman* in Canada; No 4472 surmounts a 1 in 100 climb near Cedars, Quebec, on the journey from Montreal to Kingston on September 28, 1970. [C. W. R. Bowman

Carlisle leaving the latter point at 19.30 on the return run. As events turned out, the A3 worked right through to Dumfries, but we were unaware of this change and travelled more miles than was necessary. However, the purpose of our journey was achieved. On that mellow Cumberland evening, we heard the beat of *Flying Scotman's* exhaust coming up the 1 in 132 past Cotehill well before the train came into view, breasted the summit just before Low House Crossing and accelerated into the dip before Armathwaite.

Fortunately, I read every inch of type in *Railway World* (*I am glad somebody does*! ED), otherwise I might have missed the fine print of the Gainsborough Model Railway Society's advertisement in the April 1966 issue in connection with their Lincoln—Llandudno run on June 4 hauled throughout by *Flying Scotsman*. On January 7 1966, I had reserved my flight to Britain—four weeks this time, from May 16 to June 12! Coincidence again that our charter flight organizers had chosen dates that fitted a *Flying Scotsman* excursion.

In 1967 I got married. The honeymoon was arranged for Paris and then UK. The flights were reserved before the end of January and the wedding was set for May 13. When the February *Railway World* arrived, I just could not believe my good fortune. Alan Pegler and the Gainsborough Model Railway Society had unwittingly arranged things just right for me again. After a few days of the honeymoon in Paris (interesting steam at Gare du Nord!) we returned to Southern England in time for "The Norfolkman" on May 20 and "The Retford Rover" on the following day. Hadley Wood, which I had never previously visited, was chosen after a scouting tour of the Great Northern line out of London on the Friday evening. We left our temporary headquarters at the Red Lion, Radlett, in plenty of time on the Saturday morning to take up position about mid-way between Hadley North tunnel and Potters Bar tunnel. It was one of those sunless mornings, low light level but with the sky almost white. This was the last thing I wanted, because it was cool and the A3 was almost certain to give us white steam, which would not have shown up against the sky. I decided to keep well back from the mouth of Hadley North tunnel as a considerable number of people were already set up there when we arrived. A high angle was desirable and was obtained, but I shall leave readers to figure out for themselves how it was achieved at that particular location. I was achieving two more firsts on this occasion—the first sight of an A3 coming out of London on the GN main line and the first time I had seen 4472 with the second tender.

After seven miles of 1 in 200 I expected *Flying Scotsman* to be working fairly hard. I was not disappointed. There was a veritable explosion of pure white steam as the Pacific burst from the tunnel mouth and my vantage point enabled me to get a good long ciné run of the "Norfolkman" emerging from the one tunnel and entering the other, panning through with the engine as it passed below me.

And so to 1968. For the first time, *Flying Scotsman* set our holiday dates. The January 1968 *Railway World* carried the announcement of the spring tour to Norfolk on May 12, 1968, sponsored by Jane and David Harding, so, as annual holiday planning was already in progress, we worked out a route to fit in this *Flying Scotsman*-hauled excursion. We were to leave Montreal on May 9. Then came the April issue of *Railway World* with the fabulous news of the Alan Pegler/LCGB London–Edinburgh trip to commemorate the first non-stop run by *Flying Scotsman* in 1928. Naturally, this could not be missed and a hurried telephone call was made to Air Canada, who were fortunately able to change our reservations. The detailed itinerary went out of the window and a new one was worked out. Being a Scot and having never seen 4472 on the main line into Edinburgh, we decided to concentrate on the northern end of the route, because I felt that, although there had been no announcements, *Flying Scotsman* might be doing something in Scotland on May 2 and 3 between its trips from and to London.

Although I had lived in Edinburgh for nearly 26 years, I had not done much railway photography, and many good observation points are not necessarily good picture locations because of background, direction of light, etc. I thought it advisable to check the line from Portobello up to Waverley. To this end we arrived in Edinburgh on April 30 after an overnight flight to Prestwick. Of three locations I had in mind, one was unsatisfactory and the other two were prone to obstruction by an up train—remember 1964! Waverley platform end would be good, with the twin Carlton tunnels and rock face above providing background, but I did not know if the BR authorities would be having open house and my lineside permit gave no privileges in the station area. The Station Manager at Waverley was most kind and said he intended to allow enthusiasts on the platform provided the number was not too large, in addition to providing me with the scheduled arrival time and platform number. It just had to be Nos 10 and 11! I also found that 4472 was to depart for Dunfermline MPD after a reasonable interval at Waverley for photography. What luck! Light engine across the Forth Bridge!

However, the weather in the Scottish capital on May 1, 1968, was atrocious. The light was so poor that a very fast film was absolutely essential, although one must concede that the rain could have been heavier. Using my normal technique of high angle when the light is poor, I discarded all my previously selected viewpoints and made for St Andrew's House (the Government offices overlooking Waverley station), which is situated on top of the rock cliff on the North side of the railway, with its car park conveniently located on the railway side of the building. Whoever designed St. Andrew's House must have had railway enthusiasts in mind, because, although the wall on the railway side of the car park is at least 10 ft high, a flight of steps leads up to a small observation deck with a 3 ft parapet to keep people from going over the edge. It is a long way down to Waverley! Only two other chaps joined me, so we had grandstand seats. Tension mounted as 17.35 approached. A considerable crowd had gathered at the East end of several platforms, mainly No 10. All ears were straining to catch a rumble from the Carlton tunnel as soon as the route indicator board showed SM, no colour-light signal aspects being visible from our position. Because of the broken rail and goods loop incidents, already well publicised in the railway periodicals, the arrival was about 10 min late but *Flying Scotsman* emerged from the tunnel in grand style after storming up the 1 in 78 from St. Margarets. This was indeed a triumphant occasion and the liberal use of the whistle all the way into Platforms 10 and 11 gave an indication of the footplate crew's exuberance. We left immediately for South Queensferry to get the Forth Bridge shots. At about 18.30 *Flying Scotsman* steamed across the bridge, 156 ft above high water mark, a giant dwarfed by the massive structural members of the double cantilevers and suspended spans. If only there had been sunshine!

John Murdoch and I teamed up once again on May 4 for the A3's return to London. Being somewhat greedy we wanted to see *Flying Scotsman* twice, but a check at Saughton Junction box in the morning revealed that the light engine arrival in Edinburgh was not early enough to let us get pictures west of Edinburgh, collect our wives and drive to Cockburnspath bank which I consider to be a particularly good location. So with an overcast morning becoming steadily sunnier we agreed that it was better to allow a cushion for unforeseen traffic delay on the A1 and be sure of getting to Cockburnspath in plenty of time. The delay did not materialise and we arrived at Penmanshiel Tunnel before the 14.00 Edinburgh–London: *Flying Scotsman* was booked away from Waverley at 14.20, so we were absolutely certain that we were in time. Cockburnspath is the most notable climb between Edinburgh and Newcastle at 1 in 96 for just over four miles, with the above mentioned tunnel within a mile of the summit. We were surprised to find only a handful of enthusiasts in the vicinity, but this enabled us to obtain photographs which would perhaps be indistinguishable from 1938 pictures were it not for the second tender. Quite frankly we had expected the lineside to be densely populated that afternoon.

By this time the weather was as perfect as one could wish for—sunny, warm, no wind. At 15.04 we heard the crisp three-cylinder beat coming up the hill, and then, apple-green livery gleaming in the sunlight, 4472 swept round the bend, under the little overbridge down the line, literally roared past us and finally disappeared into Penmanshiel tunnel. Another four pictures and a good, although short, recording in the bag. Our wives were almost as ecstatic as we were!

The 1969 meeting with *Flying Scotsman* took place in considerably different circumstances from those originally envisaged. The Pacific had, in fact, crossed the Atlantic! A trip to the Netherlands to attend an International Congress scheduled for early October suggested two weeks holiday in the UK immediately in advance and consequently my annual trip home was too late for any of the runs by *Flying Scotsman* and the engine sailed from Liverpool on the *Saxonia* on the day that we left Montreal. The timing of the Congress could not have been less suitable since 4472 started the US tour in Boston on October 8 and we arrived back in Montreal on October 13. The Boston and Hartford areas, being the closest points on the tour route to my home in Montreal, would have been the logical places to go in pursuit but various commitments kept me in Montreal until October 24 by which time the train had penetrated southward to the Baltimore area —a good bit farther away! The tour schedule indicated that the train would be in Baltimore from October 23–25 and on Sunday the 26th it was to make a short run of only 38 miles to Washington where there would be a further two-day stop. This did not look like much action for 1,200 miles of travel from Canada. However, on October 29, 4472 was booked to run 386 miles to Charlotte, North Carolina. With good roads following generally the same route as the railway this looked promising for following the train over a considerable distance.

My good friend, Omer Lavallée, of CP Rail, was to accompany me and we decided to allocate three days of our remaining holidays to the pursuit. Omer had already seen 4472 at Hartford, Connecticut, but not in action. The plan was to drive to Washington on October 28, chase the train for a fair part of its 386 miles trip on the following day and return to Canada on the Thursday—a total of perhaps 1,400 miles of driving. This presented no problem with two drivers and a fast car. We made a check a few days before leaving to be certain that we had the correct schedule for the exhibition train and our usually reliable source confirmed that this was so.

The weather had been ghastly in Montreal for the whole of the previous week and we were hoping it would be better to the South. When I drove away from the house on October 28 at 05.40 there was some light cloud of the kind that promises a fine day. Omer was duly picked up and we headed South through the Adirondack Mountains, had a second breakfast near Albany, New York, stopped only once more for food and fuel and drew up in front of the Union Station in Washington, DC at 16.45. We had covered the 594.4 miles in 8 hr 50 min at an average speed of 67.3 mph, almost entirely on dual carriageways, the bulk of which were toll roads. The weather was gorgeous.

On the way down I had jokingly said to Omer that it would be a bit infuriating if the schedule had been changed at the last minute. He made comforting noises which could have been interpreted as "Don't be ridiculous! They couldn't possibly change now." Granted, changes did seem highly unlikely when one remembers that the train was on an exhibition tour for business men and the public and would have been advertised in advance.

We made our way to the information desk and enquired where we would find *Flying Scotsman*. The kindly old gentleman at the desk said that it would be somewhere around Salisbury, North Carolina, as it had left Washington that morning at 07.00. So it had happened! The schedule had been changed. Omer gave me a questioning look. What did I think we should do? Salisbury is 330 miles from Washington and the time was not quite 17.00. I said we were going to Salisbury. Omer's face lit up and he exclaimed "I was hoping you would say that". The Station Master's Office was most helpful in providing us with details of the following day's run which we were assured would not be altered!

We had intended to go through the exhibition cars of the train at Washington and in case it closed to the public at 17.00 or 17.30 (assuming it had been there) we wasted no time in parking the car. There was a space outside the station which could have been construed as either a "No Parking" area or "For Permit Holders Only". I felt that the position was far enough from any of the signs that we would not get a parking ticket. So after hearing that 4472 had departed, we had a bite to eat in the station and headed back to the car. Imagine our surprise when we saw no fewer than three policemen standing beside the car! Omer, who is fluently bilingual, wondered what we should do. I told him to talk to them in French! Seriously, however, I felt that by being polite we had nothing to fear. At least it hadn't been towed away, which happens not infrequently in North America. As we reached the car one policeman said "Good evening, sir. Does your car have disc brakes on all wheels?" . . .!!!! I said that it had. One of them was puzzled by the fact that he could not see the rear discs through the wire wheels, but I explained that they were mounted inboard alongside the differential.

BELOW: The attraction of *Flying Scotsman* is well demonstrated by this photograph of the engine when it stopped at Ruabon on an excursion to Chester and North Wales in 1964. [E. N. Kneale

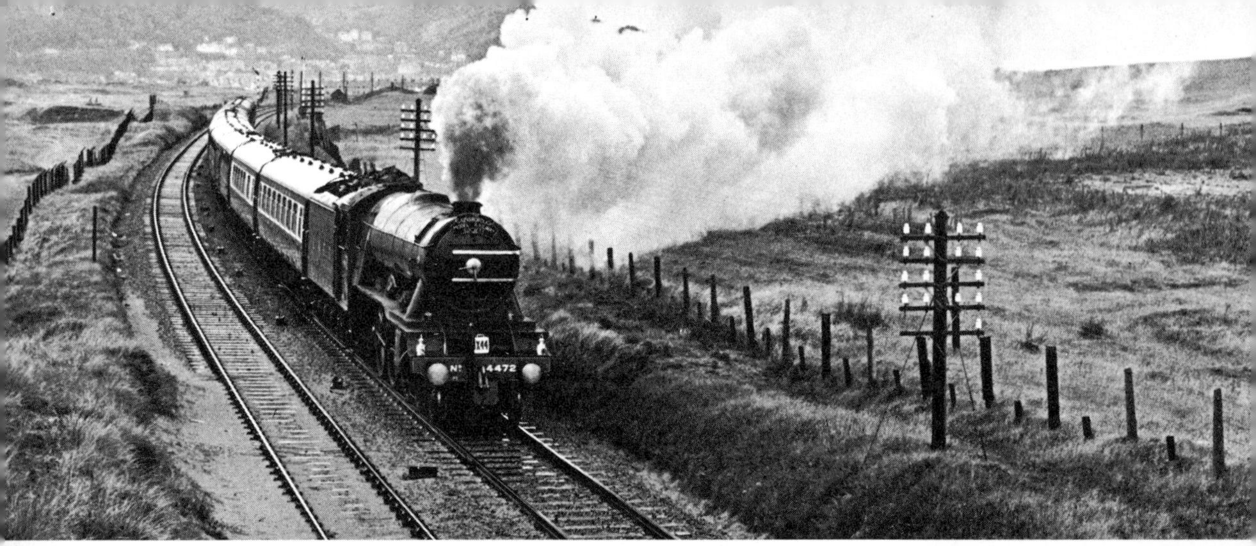
No 4472

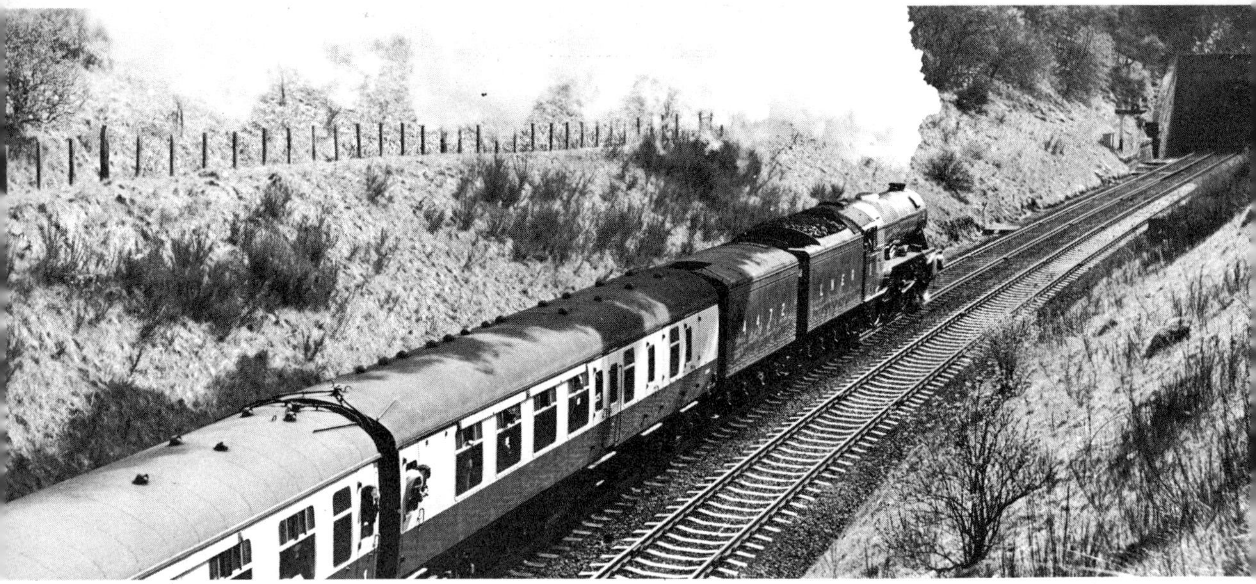

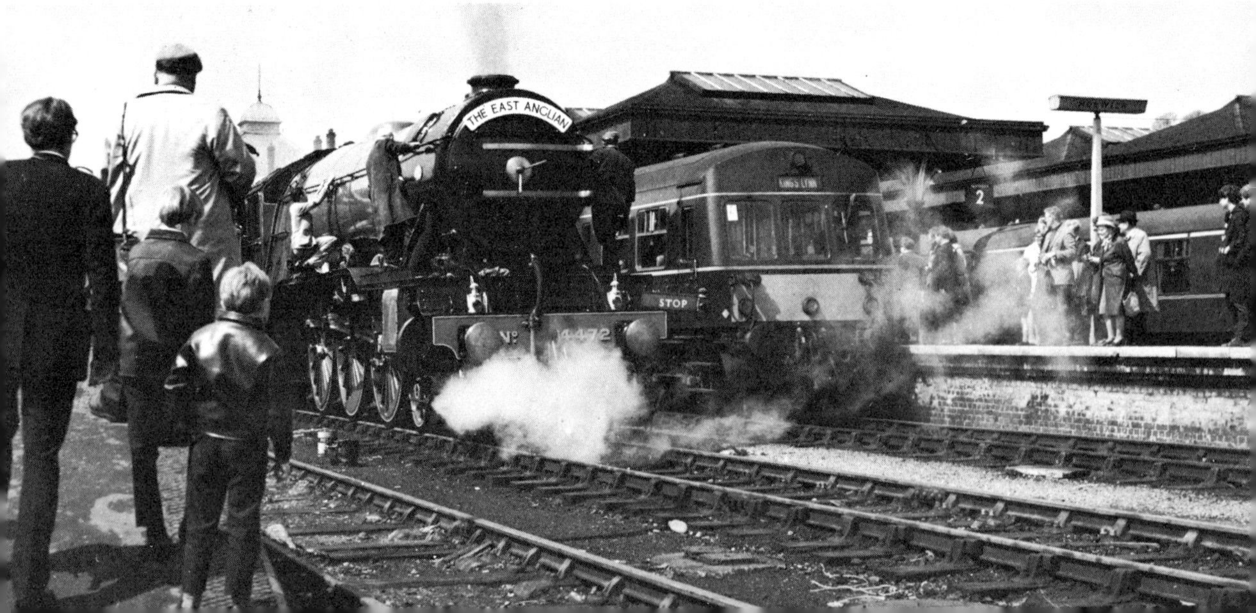
THE EAST ANGLIAN
No 4472
STOP
2

LEFT: On a wet evening, No. 4472 runs through the sand dunes near Llandudno with a return excursion to Lincoln on June 4, 1966.
[C. W. R. Bowman

RIGHT: *Flying Scotsman* on display at Hartford, Connecticut, during its North American tour. [H. A. Edmonson

LEFT: *Flying Scotsman* returns from Edinburgh to London after its non-stop run four days earlier and is seen approaching Penmanshiel Tunnel on May 4, 1968.
[C. W. R. Bowman

RIGHT: No 4472 is hoisted on to the *Saxonia* for the start of its North American tour in 1969. [Rodney Wildsmith

LEFT: No 4472 was given special attention by the staff at Norwich after its arrival with an excursion from Doncaster on May 6, 1967. [G. R. Mortimer

No mention of illegal parking! They were merely interested in the car. It should perhaps be mentioned at this point that my pursuit vehicle is a Jaguar E-type, and they had not seen one close up before. An amiable conversation ensued and we were joined by a fourth policeman. Of course, they were rather astounded when we told them why we were in Washington.

After chatting for about 15 min, we ploughed our way out of Washington in the evening rush hour and put 260 miles behind us with one stop before arriving at Durham, North Carolina, at 23.10 where we went on shed for the night. Omer suggested having the motel office call us at 06.30. I'm afraid I was ruthless—call at 05.30 and departure as soon as possible thereafter.

The weather was again perfect as we drew away from Durham at 05.50. Silver Arrow (the E-type) sped along Interstate Highway 85 and brought us to Salisbury at 07.15, 15 min before 4472 was booked away. We were like a pair of excited schoolboys. There was *Flying Scotsman* in the station, ready to leave, gleaming in the low morning sunlight at the head of the nine coach train—a brake second, the five exhibition cars, Pullman cars *Isle of Thanet* and *Lydia*, and the observation car—all in Pullman colours. There were a number of people around, but no milling mass of spectators and few enthusiasts. So here it was that I climbed onto the footplate of this beloved A3 for the first time. At this point the train was travelling on the Southern Railway, so 4472 had a Southern (US) crew as well as the BR men. I mentioned that we had just driven down from Montreal whereupon the BR driver (from Doncaster, naturally) said I sounded as if I had just arrived from Edinburgh! This city was correct but the arrival was 16 years ago!

The A3 threw a tall plume into the still, cool morning air as the day's run to Gainesville, Georgia, started. A stop was to be made at Charlotte, 40 miles away, to pick up the train staff (the girls!) who had spent the night there, Salisbury presumably being a more suitable stabling point for the train from a railway operating point of view. Here was our first opportunity to get ahead of the train with ease and perhaps have breakfast. We did, shortly before 09.00, having already driven 161 miles.

Our major difficulty was lack of knowledge of the area so we had no pre-chosen photographic viewpoints. There was also the reluctance to stray very far from the excellent dual carriageways without which we would have achieved very little. Every time we left the dual 4472 would likely be gaining on us and we never knew exactly how many minutes we were ahead. However, as will be seen, with Omer's fine navigation, coupled with an assumed 50 miles per hour average for 4472 (single track main line), the Official Guide to the Railways (which provided mileages) and the reliability of the E-type we really had nothing to worry about.

After two attempts at photographing *Flying Scotsman* on the move, we soon approached Spartanburg at 11.00, a moderately sized town where 4472 had a booked stop for servicing until 12.30. Spartanburg station was a hive of activity when we arrived. With the train staff girls on the platform wearing their mini-kilts it was a wonder anyone was bothering about *Flying Scotsman*! There did not appear to be many railway enthusiasts around, perhaps because it was a working day, but a good number of townspeople were on hand. The girls were posed in front of *Flying Scotsman*, probably for the benefit of the local news photographers.

I suspect the photographers were more interested in the girls because very little of the A3's front end was still visible—one buffer, siren, bell, headlight and just a trace of smokebox door. After all there were eight girls on the running plate and buffer beam and four more on the track with the piper! Contrasted against the black steel were red minikilts matched to red sweaters, green minikilts paired with either little green sweaters or white blouses and a couple of red minis topped by navy blue sweaters. Flying Scotsman behaved like a gentleman until someone in the cab pulled the siren cord! Feminine hands were hastily applied to feminine ears and the expressions told us that a few startled shrieks were emitted—but never heard.

Taking a 20 min lead on the train, we headed away from Spartanburg following the line on secondary roads. After crossing twice road and rail diverged and we had no sight of the track for a few miles. Taking the next road south we descended into a valley and on rounding a curve came upon a delightful long trestle bridge near Greer. Like many bridges in North America there was no parapet to obstruct one's view of the wheels. We took up position and waited. If 4472 left Spartanburg at 12.30 as scheduled it should have passed us no later than 12.45. At about 12.50 Omer made one of those soul-shattering statements. I wonder if this is the right line! I gave him a rather withering look and reminded him that he was the expert on American railways. If this wasn't the Southern main line, what was it? We comforted ourselves by confirming that we had been running with the line to the south, had turned south and here we were. The only other line that we knew of in the area was definitely to the north of us. Shortly after 13.00 *Flying Scotsman's* deep siren was heard away to the east, then closer but a little to the south. There must be a long curve approaching the bridge, we thought. Then again, definitely due south now—and worried glances were exchanged! Our worst fears were confirmed by the fourth whistle—fainter and away to the south-west. Our bridge must have been on a branch (that's the problem with single track main lines). Omer's "you can't win 'em all" was little comfort. Where now?

4472 was building up a good lead on us as we had some distance to go on secondary roads to get back to the fast highway. Earlier in the day we had noticed that a small town called Westminster was on the railway, close to the border between South Carolina and Georgia. This was another good English-sounding name to go with Salisbury. It was now a little more than an hour's drive ahead, Omer calculated. His estimate was that I would reach Westminster at 14.15 and that *Flying Scotsman* would pass through not earlier than 14.30. As it turned out, the actual times were 14.20 and 14.43 respectively. We found the station quickly (there is only one) and although there was no outstanding view-point close by it was quite pleasant and we did not want to go seeking something which might be no better, with the risk of missing the train. The disappointment at Greer was still uppermost! So we were rewarded by the sight of 4472 travelling at speed through this small South Carolina town—no whistles this time, but it was cool enough to show steam from the chimney.

The train conductor had told me at Spartanburg that pictures were to be taken in the vicinity of Toccoa, a few miles over the border in Georgia. He did not know if there would be a stop but expected a bit of slow running. We had no idea of the gradients, but this slowing might have been designed to allow photography while the engine was subsequently accelerating. So Toccoa area was next and only 18 miles away. We had to move. About half-way is the South Carolina–Georgia border formed at this point by a widening of the Savannah River known as Hartwell Reservoir. At this point the desirability of scouting the line in advance was brought home to us. As Silver Arrow streaked over the causeway carrying the road across the reservoir, we looked upstream and saw the finest scenic view that had presented itself all day. The railway crossed the water on a multi-span girder bridge, with a beautiful background of hills, and the bridge was just far enough from the causeway that our telephoto lenses would have given a side-on shot of 4472 and perhaps part of the train. The degree of beauty was such that Omer commented that it looked rather like Glenfinnan. It did, too, apart from the difference in bridge types and the expanse of water. We had not yet caught up with *Flying Scotsman*, but if only we had known about this spot it would have been much better than Westminster.

We overtook the train as we were entering Toccoa and could see the steam against the trees on the hillside. We got glimpses of *Flying Scotsman* and either the gradient was very steep or the engine was accelerating away from the brief stop or check. Our maps showed the road making a big loop southward just west of Toccoa which led us to believe that this was following valleys to get through a range of hills. This proved to be the case, but the railway did not accompany us. So the line either looped to the north or worse still perhaps the rail route went straight via a tunnel. The E-type stormed up a long winding climb through the hills, its occupants now beginning to feel that the mandatory loop southward had lost us any slight advantage we had. Still in a cutting ourselves, we reached the summit and found a pall of black smoke hanging over the road. From the fast glimpse we got, it was a rather unusual location—the Southern Railway in a very deep rock cutting spanned by the road bridge which itself linked two quite deep road cuttings. *Flying Scotsman* had just passed under the bridge and was obviously working hard. I was, of course, fuming because one minute earlier at that bridge would have been marvellous. Omer remained absolutely calm! After a short sharp downhill left-hander, we found ourselves parallel to the track and the road ahead as straight as a die. Speed moved quickly to three figures and we left the train behind. On slowing for a curve at the end of this straight we noticed a small road going towards the track—only about 200 yd away. We decided to take a quick look. The cutting was shallow, trees lined the top of both banks, a bridge spanned the track and the sun was well placed. 4472 was no more than a mile away and laying a great trail of smoke, the like of which I have never seen coming out of a British locomotive chimney before. *Flying Scotsman* barked towards us for what seemed an age, but could not have been much more than two minutes, providing for its background this great dark grey pall. Speed was only about 30 mph so the gradient must have been very severe. Here then was the A3 in full cry, by far the most rewarding sight of the day. Anything else would have been an anticlimax. So we watched *Flying Scotsman* out of sight, still climbing toward Cornelia, Georgia. It was now 15.20 and *Flying Scotsman* had only about 30 more miles to go and our mileage for the day was 350 of which the pursuit accounted for 254. So we declared ourselves well satisfied, gave thanks for the glorious weather, the super highways and Silver Arrow's flawless assistance and started to think about our return. We were 1,200 miles from home. Up to this point I had done all the driving, so I handed over to Omer, and we pointed the Arrow Northwards. The run through the Great Smoky Mountains was uneventful and we clocked a further 232 miles before stopping for the night at Bristol, which straddles the Tennessee–Virginia state boundary.

A rather fascinating thing happened at the motel. Although it was nearly 23.00 and we had been on the go since before 06.00 I turned on the television while getting ready for bed. One channel was showing a film which I had seen a number of years ago. The name escaped me but I recognized Kenneth More as the principal actor. I had to know what this was so we watched for a bit. Then there were some scenes in a train which was eventually shown steaming into—of all places—Waverley! Then it all came back—*The* 39 *Steps*. We waited to see the shot of the A4 being stopped on the Forth Bridge and then turned in. A fitting end to a Gresley day.

We slept late the following morning and were on the road, having had breakfast for a change, at 07.40. We reached Montreal at 23.40 after covering 924 miles. So ended a hectic but worthwhile three-day trip. For the statistically minded the following facts may be interesting.

Distance	October 28	855 miles
	October 29	582 miles
	October 30	924 miles
Total distance		2361 miles
Petrol		110 gallons
Fuel consumption		21.5 mpg
No of photographs (including the mini-kilts)		30

One might wonder why we were not using maps which showed the railways, instead of road maps and the Official Guide to the Railways giving station names. Unfortunately, in North America there are no maps that we know of available at newsagents and bookstalls, of the type published by Bartholomews (eg 6 miles to the inch) which would have been ideal. The only solution would have been government topographic maps (4 miles to the inch) and ordering in advance would have been necessary. We'll do this next time!

In 1970 *Flying Scotsman* came to Canada and for once the pursuit did not involve any flying—either in the air or on the ground. 4472 did a tour in the US in June/July and another in Canada from August to October. There had been a considerable change in the route. First it was intended to run from Texas to California and up the US West Coast into Canada and then right across Canada from west to east with a dip into the US Mid-West states. At least one US railway was not willing to authorise steam running and the revised route went up the middle of the US south to north from Texas to Wisconsin terminating on July 19 at the National RR Museum in Green Bay, Wisconsin. One of the permanent exhibits here is A4 60008 *Dwight D. Eisenhower*. Pity about California as I have relatives there and we could have arranged our holidays to follow the train north to Vancouver.

The second part of the 1970 Tour experienced several revisions and it was not until August 10 that the dates were reasonably certain. Even then a schedule footnote said "Times shown are not firm. Schedule subject to change." Hmmm! After running from Green Bay, via Chicago, *Flying Scotsman* entered Canada by way of the St Clair tunnel at Sarnia, Ontario on August 20. Strange that 4472 should first set wheel on Canadian track actually below the surface! In fact below water as well, as the international boundary at this point is formed by the St Clair River. The whole of the A3's sojourn in Canada was on CN metals.

I had decided that I could see the A3 in action twice in the Montreal area, where I live, but I was also prepared to spend a day away from the office to catch the Sarnia–Toronto run on August 21, 1970. Knowing this route well, I decided that I would like to tape the engine on the 1 in 119 climb from Bayview Junction to Burlington, Ontario, some 35 miles west of Toronto. There are no outstanding viewpoints on this climb and photographs would be more or less record shots rather than pictorial.

At 16.10 on the afternoon of August 20, 1970 the CN Turbo slid out of Montreal's Central station with myself as one of the Toronto-bound passengers. My wife Patricia, who had gone to Toronto earlier in the week by car, picked me up at that end and we drove to Burlington. The following morning dawned near-perfect—sunny, mild, with a very light breeze. We made a precautionary call at Burlington station to check if there were any last minute changes to the schedule. Everything at that time (09.15) was as planned—dep. Sarnia 10.00, arr. Toronto 14.00, an easy run of 174 miles based on an average running speed of approximately 50 mph.

A stop had, however, been arranged at Burlington to pick up a press party who were to travel on board to Toronto. This was an added bonus as the stop would enable us to move from our pre-selected location to some point east of Burlington while the train was at a stand. The extra viewpoint would have to be in a built-up area so we spent part of the forenoon selecting a site and checking best access and driving times between the two. The viewpoint on the climb from Bayview Junction is quite close to the main highway, and we would be able to regain the car quickly, which in this instance was Patricia's Austin 1100—a little slower than the E-type.

Although *Flying Scotsman* was not due to pass us until somewhere around 12.45, we set up at 11.30 and photographed everything that went by while waiting. Some cumulus was drifting over the sun by this time and the breeze was freshening but we had no complaints about weather. We saw only one other photographer on this part of the line—the wife of some poor chap who couldn't get off work. She had apparently been given very clear instructions—get pictures! In her haste to ensure that she did not miss the train, she had left the ignition key in her car and having realised this was rather concerned about the possibility of it being stolen. Having already walked a good half-mile down the line, she was reluctant to go back. Patricia assured her that it would be more worthwhile to get the *Flying Scotsman* pictures! As she went further down the line I hope she had a good supply of patience. Several trains had passed, but at 12.30 a freight came growling up the hill behind 6,600 hp of diesel power in the form of CN 3208/5030. As the caboose clicked by slowly, the conductor called down—"one hour behind". He knew what we were there for. Whether he meant that 4472 was one hour behind his train or behind schedule did not really matter because it was much the same thing. However, it was 14.00 before we saw *Flying Scotsman* for the first time in Canada. She came up the bank in fine style with just a slight grey haze emanating from the chimney. I had fitted one camera with the 300 mm lens for a head-on shot initially and having taken this, I moved off smartly over a flat area south of the track and was able to get four shots from the side. Patricia was manning the tape-recorder and I was pleased to hear some enterprising chap on the footplate give a long-short on the LNER whistle as he approached.

Flying Scotsman's lateness was not due to any mechanical or operating difficulties. It was just the fact that so many people had turned out at towns and villages along the route that a few unscheduled stops were made to reward their interest with a longer look at the A3 and her train. It also transpired later that the slow exit from Burlington was due to bridge construction in the vicinity. This had necessitated manual operation of all signals within about a two mile radius for some two weeks and aspects for signals affected had to be regarded as equivalent to hand signals by flagmen.

I particularly wanted to ascertain the origin of the engine's "new" American whistle, but I could see no indication of this on the device itself when we had a close look at one of the exhibition stops. It was mounted, as the siren had been in 1969, on the right-hand side of the smokebox. Mr Pegler was in the Observation Car when we reached that end of the train and from him I found that Mr W. Graham Claytor, Jr, President of the Southern Railway System in the US, had considered the siren too large and for a short portion of the 1969 tour a chime whistle about 100 years old had been loaned for use on Flying Scotsman. Subsequently, Mr Claytor, an enthusiast as well as a professional railwayman, provided the present Southern whistle.

But the interesting news was still to come. Mr Pegler mentioned that he would like to keep the locomotive in Canada over the coming winter and "do something" here in 1971. He also felt it would be most appropriate if the last part of the 1970 tour could be modified to finish in London, Ontario, a city of some 200,000 population. This possibility, and a winter storage location, were being negotiated with CN, at the time of writing.

I am greatly indebted to the many people who have contributed to those grand experiences that I have described and which I shall treasure for the rest of my life. My thanks are due to Mr Alan Pegler for preserving the engine in the first place, to the sponsors of the runs for their efforts in organizing the trips and their admirable choice of dates (!), to BR for providing me with lineside and shed permits, to the drivers, firemen, cleaners, fitters and other BR staff who have contributed in their own diverse ways to the success of so many runs, to the Station Manager at Waverley and my Running Foreman friends in Edinburgh, George Cree (then at St Margarets) and Willie Noble at Dalry Road, for their generous assistance. I am particularly grateful to James Brown, CN Co-ordinator for the Flying Scotsman tour in Canada, Ian MacDonald, also of CN, and Omer Lavallée, CP Rail, for providing me with a great deal of helpful information. Finally I am more than indebted to my wife, Patricia, for tolerating my hobby and being willing to spend annual holidays doing railway photography and recording.

The 2 - 4 - 0 portrayed

C. HAMILTON ELLIS

At the end of the last century, one could see the supposedly archaic 2-4-0 express locomotive successfully heading the most important passenger and mail trains in Great Britain, and in the Kingdom of the Netherlands; to a lesser extent in Ireland, and scarcely anywhere else in the world. The type was almost unknown in North America, though, to be sure, the *J. W. Bowker* has long survived its Virginia & Truckee Railroad. Of "modern" examples, Bavaria could show only the scarcely numerous Bremen class, dating from the late 'eighties, (*Bremen* survives in the *Verkehrsmuseum* at Nurenberg), Russia had some ancient oddments still liable to turn up on important trains east of Brest-Litovsk; France and Belgium had—in different forms—both elongated the type into the 2-4-2, to give improved steadiness in France and to support an enormous Belpaire firebox in Belgium. Abroad, as suggested, only in the Netherlands was the type still in honour.

The Holland Railway used Borsig 2-4-0 engines with Belpaire fireboxes and outside Walschaerts gear, but already it was discarding these in favour of the inside-cylindered 4-4-0 of Sharp Stewart inspiration. The Dutch State Railways had a beautiful 7 ft 2-4-0 class by Beyer Peacock, but nevertheless had just begun to enlarge and elongate this into a 4-4-0, producing something almost suggesting a Great Western Badminton.

But at home, the London & North Western was still cheerfully heading West Coast expresses with Webb "Jumbos". The Great Eastern class T 19 went romping off to Yarmouth and the Norfolk Coast, ere the Claud Hamiltons displaced it, and there were others, even Conner veterans of the Caledonian heading the "Postals" north of Perth.

Of English railways, the first to discard the single-driver express engine had been the London & South Western under Joseph Beattie and the North Eastern under Edward Fletcher. In each case, the large-wheeled 2-4-0 succeeded it. There were different consequences. On the South Western, even the 2-4-0 ceased to be built after 1875, while the North Eastern, in the 1880s, saw a revival of single driving wheels, with much bigger bogie

ABOVE: Great Eastern 2-4-0 No 735 is portrayed alongside GNR 0-4-2 No 112 in this painting by the author.

engines, under the influence of steam sanding gear, the usefulness of which had lately been shown by the Midland Railway (another single-revival line.)

Yet at that time, some of the very best work on the North Eastern was being done by 2-4-0 express engines (McDonnell's 4-4-0 with its swing-link bogie had somewhat flopped). The engines were the later ones of Edward Fletcher, and their derivatives known as "Tennants" (after Henry Tennant, General Manager, during an interregnum on the Locomotive Department). Both the older engines, dating from the 1870s, and the synthetic "Tennants", were extremely useful during the fiercely competitive running of the late 1880s. But even at the beginning of the 1920s they were still to be seen. One recalls from 1920 going to Harrogate behind a Fletcher seven-footer, and at York seeing a "Tennant" bringing in an express from Scarborough to Leeds, that giving a London connection by an express which followed it in from Middlesbrough, on the same platform.

Scarborough expresses long provided a happy exercise for these great 2-4-0 engines with their 7ft driving wheels and most elegant outlines. The term "great" is used in its finer sense, for even to our youthful eyes in those days, they were not very big engines. Affection is behind the painting of my picture of a Scarborough express, as running somewhat earlier, on that lovely sinuous line by Castle Howard and Kirkham Abbey.

In the early 1900s, the train would have a Refreshment Car, or Refreshment Saloon, improvised from an elderly Pullman sleeper which had become the North Eastern company's property. First-class passengers were admitted of course, and third-class on payment of half-a-crown if there was room for them. One such is the second vehicle in my picture. The Fletcher engine has acquired a Worsdell boiler, with which all the survivors had been equipped in your author's young days, and for long previously. A note, however, on this: York Museum happily contains No 910 of the Fletchers, dating from 1875. She *appears* to be in mint condition, and so steamed in the Railway Centenary procession of 1925. My old friend and fellow-traveller Richard Inness told me the delightful restoration story: "Oh," he said, "we could put back her old outline and finish all right. But the levers and spring balances don't really do anything. We put a single Ross pop valve in the casing." One can think of many less plausible prevarications than that, such as wooden dummies and other horrors.

Midland 2-4-0 engines had the greatest staying power of the lot, were they Kirtley's or Johnson's. One of the former—albeit not an express engine—plodded doggedly through the Hitler war, having been old during the Kaiser's, and no-longer-young during the South African one. But for my second picture I have chosen a London & North Western "Jumbo", whose design dates back to 1873 with *Precedent* and whose race has survived in *Hardwicke*, presently at Clapham. My choice is *Courier*, for sentimental reasons, and I have put her beside Bassenthwaite Lake on the Cockermouth, Keswick & Penrith Railway for aesthetic ones, though that lovely place was the more likely habitat of the 6ft version, and of the 0-6-0 "Cauliflowers". (One could see *Saddleback* below Saddleback.) *Courier* was built in 1877 and, according to a minute stamping on her nameplates, rebuilt in February 1896.

So much has been authoritatively written about the 6ft 6in "Jumbos" on the London & North Western Railway that summary seems superfluous. They were small, short, severely plain, noisy little engines, like many others on the LNWR. They were extremely reliable. They were strong. (*Hardwicke* fell off a bridge in Birmingham after an encounter with a Midland train when quite new; and happily survived to make a record run in the racing of 1895.) Well, there they were, and here are my pictures, and though North Eastern No 329, and North Western *Courier* have gone, we still have NER No 910 and LNWR *Hardwicke*.

Two more paintings by the author; the one above shows LNWR *Courier* at Bassenthwaite and below, North Eastern 2-4-0 No 329 with a Scarborough Express.

M E R
329

ABOVE: Standard Class 5 4-6-0 No 73029 climbs past Upwey Wishing Well Halt with a parcels train on May 9, 1967. The town of Weymouth can be seen in the centre background. [Derek Cross

Weymouth in the last 20 years

S. A. ROCKSBOROUGH SMITH

WEYMOUTH as a holiday resort dates from the reign of King George III, whose statue stands in the town. The town has an ideal situation, from the west there is Portland Bill and Harbour, then Weymouth Harbour, with the shortest crossing to the Channel Islands, and the Pier. Then come the beaches of Greenhill, Lodmoor, Overcombe and Bowleaze; the bay is bounded to the east by cliffs leading out to White Nose. Weymouth Bay is sandy and quite shallow at high or low tide.

Weymouth was first reached by rail in 1857. Weymouth, or Budmouth, was a centre for social life and excitement to those who lived on Thomas Hardy's Egdon Heath; to the directors of the Great Western Railway, at Paddington, it must have seemed rather remote.

Weymouth has never formed part of a railway coastal complex, as exists in Kent and Sussex, the Portsmouth area or Torbay, but was reached by a long, thin line of communication, known as the Wilts, Somerset & Weymouth Railway. It left the Bristol main line at Thingley Junction, near Chippenham, and passed through Melksham, Westbury and Yeovil.

Weymouth is historically a GWR town, but the first railway into the area was the Southampton & Dorchester. This reached Dorchester in 1847, and was planned to strike west to Bridport and Exeter. It is well known how the LSWR was turned by the Wilts, Somerset & Weymouth and built a sharply curved spur to join that line at Dorchester Junction. LSW trains entered Weymouth in 1857 on the same day as those of the Wilts, Somerset & Weymouth, which was built on the broad gauge, but converted in 1874.

Dorchester South station shows its origin to this day. At first all stopping trains had to reverse into or out of its platforms. A new down platform was built on the curve in 1879; but up stopping trains had to reverse into the original platform until June 1970, when a new up platform on the curve was eventually brought into use. On the curve to Dorchester Junction there is a 15 mph speed restriction.

The Castle Cary–Weymouth line

In 1906 the GWR West of England main line was opened via Newbury and Westbury to Taunton. The Weymouth line effectively became a branch from Castle Cary. The whole of this line was in GWR hands until 1948, and at Weymouth Southern trains had their own arrival and departure platforms on the outer edges of the GWR station. In April 1950 the line from Dorchester to Castle Cary became part of the Southern Region, but the SR did not have operating control of the line until the beginning of 1958. In June 1963 the boundary was redrawn just north of Dorchester West station. Weymouth is now the furthest point from London in the whole of the Southern Region.

The Weymouth line leaves the main line at Castle Cary under a road bridge by a stark, pale-coloured signal box. The first place of importance is Yeovil (Pen Mill), where the up line has a platform on both sides. At Pen Mill the line to Yeovil Town (now closed) diverges to the right; shortly afterwards the Weymouth line runs parallel to the double track of the Yeovil Junction–Yeovil Town branch, and then through a bridge under the Waterloo–Exeter line east of Yeovil Junction.

Originally there was no connection between the WR line and the SR Yeovil Junction–Yeovil Town branch. One was built at Yeovil South Junction during the second world war, known as the wartime connection, and enabled a train to run direct from Pen Mill to Yeovil Junction. It saw no regular passenger service except for a year from 1967–68, after Yeovil Town was closed to passengers, and the Yeovil Junction auto train was diverted to Pen Mill. In May 1968 even this service was withdrawn.

During summer 1965 two Saturday expresses used the wartime connection, the 11.45 Paddington–Ilfracombe and Bude, and the 10.45 Ilfracombe–Paddington. They replaced the SR trains from Waterloo, but used this route only for one season. The purpose was to avoid reversal at Exeter St David's.

Beyond Yeovil the Weymouth line enters Dorset and after Yetminster starts a climb of some three miles through Chetnole to Evershot; Chetnole bank is 1 in 51 at its steepest point. Any load over nine coaches usually required banking assistance, but even in the 1950s few full length trains climbed the bank except in the summer months. Every summer until 1959 the Channel Islands Boat Express ran on weekdays from Paddington to Weymouth Quay, and on summer Saturdays in the 1950s a number of trains used to take bankers. The engines were provided by Yeovil shed, and were WR 45XX or 57XX tanks, or SR Class U 2-6-0s; they banked through Evershot tunnel and dropped off in Evershot station.

Evershot signal box was closed during the winter of 1964/5. The following summer the Saturday 10.45 Wolverhampton–Weymouth was still regularly steam-hauled, and needed assistance on the bank. An NBL class 22 diesel (D63XX) was attached to the front at Yeovil and piloted the train through to Maiden Newton. Trains not booked to call at Maiden Newton or Dorchester, took the pilot right through to Weymouth.

At Maiden Newton the Bridport branch, worked under the one-train-operation regulations, leaves the Weymouth line in the up direction.

The next place of importance is Dorchester West; between here and Castle Cary the line has been singled and divided into three sections, with loops at Yeovil and Maiden Newton. Castle Cary to Maiden Newton is worked by electric token in two sections and from there to Dorchester by tokenless block. The singling was carried out in May and June 1968. Dorchester West signalbox was closed in March 1968 and this end of the single line is controlled by Dorchester Junction.

Despite the present-day unimportance of the WR line, it still has the appearance of the main line at Dorchester Junction, where the SR comes in from the left on a sharp curve. The summit of the line between Dorchester and Weymouth is at Bincombe Tunnel. At the north end of the tunnel begins the descent to Weymouth, 1 in 50 at its steepest, easing to 1 in 74 through Radipole. Coming out of a second shorter tunnel, and passing the closed Upwey Wishing Well Halt, there is a magnificent view of Weymouth Bay and Portland. Upwey & Broadwey used to be known as Upwey Junction, because of the Abbotsbury branch which was closed in 1952.

Weymouth

Just after Radipole Halt down trains pass Weymouth shed on the left. Weymouth was a WR shed until the beginning of 1958. Until June 1957 the SR had its own shed at Dorchester South, on the down side, but after 1955 the shed had no allocation of its own, and was used only for servicing and stabling. In September 1958 the last Hall class 4-6-0s were transferred away from Weymouth and replaced by five Standard Class 5 4-6-0s. The first diesel shunter was allocated to Weymouth in October 1960, to begin the replacement of the 1366 class pannier tanks on the Quay tramway.

In September 1964 Weymouth became a principal shed on the SR South Western Division, and received its first allocation of Merchant Navy Pacifics. By the beginning of 1965 almost all the WR turns to and from Weymouth were covered by Hymek Class 35 diesels from Bath Road shed.

Weymouth shed closed on July 9, 1967, when the Bournemouth electrification was finally completed and the new SR timetable came into force. The table opposite shows its allocation at different times since nationalisation.

Just short of Weymouth Town station is Weymouth Junction, where the Portland branch and the line leading to the Weymouth Quay tramway diverge to the right. There was a separate signal box at Weymouth Junction until 1957, when that and the former station box were replaced by the present Weymouth signal box.

The Portland branch ran across the causeway and terminated at Easton, in the middle of Portland island. It was closed to passenger traffic in March 1952, but Melcombe Regis, the first station on the branch, remained open for a few more years, and was used as a terminus for certain trains on summer Saturdays. In summer 1956, for example, the 12.15 from Dorchester South and the 13.10 Bournemouth Central, and from the WR the 12.10 Yeovil and 13.18 Dorchester West terminated there on Saturdays. The Portland branch closed altogether in April 1965.

The Quay tramway is used by passenger, mail and perishables trains to and from the Channel Islands. It runs along the back streets of the town beside the harbour. Only the lightest of locomotives are permitted, and until May 1961 the tramway was worked by the WR 1366 0-6-0PT class. For most of the 1950s Nos 1367, 1368 and 1370 were allocated to Weymouth. Trains change engines after pulling across on to the branch, although in WR days the 08.20 Channel Islands Boat Express from Paddington changed engines on the main line at Weymouth Junction, except on summer Saturdays. The tramway engine proceeds to the Quay at walking pace, clanging a bell, carrying a sign reading "DANGER. KEEP 50 FT CLEAR", and with two or three pilotmen walking in front. The journey is usually allowed 17 min. Delays are often caused by parked cars obstructing the track, although the clearance is now marked by white lines in the road. There are also delays to road traffic where the line crosses a busy main road at Westham Bridge.

Since 1961 trains to the Quay have been worked by diesel shunters. The Quay station originally had two platforms. It was rebuilt in 1960 and a third platform added.

Bincombe Bank

In steam days practically every up train of eight coaches or more (but sometimes less), would be assisted on Bincombe bank. During the year as a whole, few of Weymouth's departures were too heavy for a single engine to handle; but in summer there was the boat train which ran each weekday from May to September, the trains of perishable traffic from the Channel Islands, fairly heavy excursion traffic and a succession of well-loaded Saturday departures, all of which needed assistance.

WR trains were always given banking assistance at the rear, while those for the Southern generally took on a pilot at the front end. The stock for departures from Weymouth Town was propelled into the platforms, often long in advance of departure time; banking engines were not allowed to be trapped in the station for long periods behind the trains, and so a train needing a banker had to pull up again almost immediately after departure for the banker to come on. This added 5 min to the time from Weymouth to

Class	*Numbers*			
	June 1950	*March 1956*	*January 1963*	*January 1967*
Merchant Navy	—	—	—	10
Castle	1	—	—	—
Hall	7	4	—	—
Modified Hall	2	1	—	—
Standard 5MT	—	—	8	4
Saint	1	—	—	—
4300	7	2	—	—
N 2-6-0	—	—	2	—
5700	1	6	7	—
5100	—	2	—	—
4500	3	2	—	—
7400	1	—	—	—
1501	1	—	—	—
5400	—	1	—	—
1400	3	3	—	—
1366	3	3	—	—
WR Diesel railcar	1	1	—	—
200 hp Diesel shunters	—	—	4	2

ABOVE: Modern style at Weymouth with Birmingham Type 3 diesel No D6527 propelling a 4TC train out of Weymouth on June 10, 1967, a few weeks before the end of steam on the SR Bournemouth—Weymouth line. [R. E. Toop

Dorchester. Boat trains did not suffer delays in attaching a banker, since they had to stop anyway to change engines.

This delay could be avoided for heavy Southern trains calling at Dorchester South, for they were normally given pilot engines, which were uncoupled when the train stopped beyond Dorchester South for reversal into the up platform. The train engine then set the train back, and the pilot as often as not crossed to the down line and returned to Weymouth immediately. Almost the only regular trains not calling at Dorchester South were the boat trains, after they had been rerouted to Waterloo at the end of 1959.

By 1963 Weymouth engines covered most of the pilot turns as well as the rear-end banking. That summer two Standard Class 4 2-6-4Ts were transferred to Weymouth shed; after a few weeks, however, they were replaced by six LMR Class 2 2-6-2Ts, and members of this class performed occasional pilot duties on the bank in the next three years.

Regular services on the Western line

The main stream of traffic on the Castle Cary–Weymouth line has always been from Bristol (Temple Meads), via Bath, Bradford-on-Avon, Trowbridge and Westbury. In the summer of 1956 there were four through trains in each direction; in the current timetable there are only two down and three up, but additional services to Bristol are provided by connection with Portsmouth line trains at Westbury.

In 1956 Paddington was a recognised London departure point for Weymouth, and a return ticket from Weymouth or Dorchester to London could be used interchangeably on the two routes. The journey from Paddington to Weymouth, via Reading, Newbury and Westbury, took about four hours. Departures from Paddington were at 12.30 and 18.00, and from Weymouth at 09.00 and 16.10. Only part of the train ran through to Weymouth. The 12.30 detached a portion at Westbury; the 18.00 ran non-stop to Newbury, and there detached a portion which stopped at stations to Trowbridge via Devizes.

But in the down direction Weymouth passengers could travel from Paddington by slip coach. The trains concerned were the 10.30 Cornish Riviera Limited and the 15.30 Paddington–Penzance. They slipped a portion, often of two coaches, at Heywood Road Junction, east of Westbury. While the main train carried on via the Westbury avoiding

ABOVE: Merchant Navy Pacific No 35012 *United States Line* waits to leave Weymouth with the 17.35 to Waterloo. On the left WR 0-6-0PT No 4624 plays with a pair of refrigerated containers. [Bryan H. Kimber

line, the slip coaches were brought to a halt at the signal box, and later hauled into Westbury station. There they were attached to the rear of an ordinary Weymouth passenger train. In summer 1956 the down "Limited" was booked to slip a coach at Heywood Road Junction at 12.02 (Saturdays excepted). The coach departed for Westbury at 12.09, arriving at 12.12, and there became part of the 11.45 Chippenham–Weymouth stopping train. But the fastest timing was by the slip coach off the 15.30 Paddington, which joined with the 16.25 Bristol semi-fast and reached Weymouth in 3 hr 27 min. This compared well with the Southern expresses from Waterloo. The only disadvantage was that Weymouth passengers were cut off from the main train, and could not use the restaurant car. The 10.30 slip was withdrawn in September 1958 and the 15.30 in January 1959.

Regular Paddington–Weymouth through services came to an end in 1960, two years after the SR took over operating control of the Castle Cary–Weymouth line. In May 1969 a through diesel multiple-unit service was introduced between Reading and Weymouth over this route, down in the evenings and leaving Weymouth at 05.48 in the up direction, but this operated only for one year.

A regular service in the 1950s was the Wolverhampton–Weymouth through train. It ran via Oxford, Didcot West Curve and Swindon, and then traversed the whole of the original Wilts, Somerset & Weymouth line from Thingley Junction. In 1956 the down train reached Weymouth at 17.14; the up train departed at 10.32. The service had operated each weekday all the year round until September 1951, when it was reduced to Saturdays only in winter. Except for summer Saturdays it was a light load. In September 1958 the winter train was withdrawn, and in the following summer it ran on Fridays and Saturdays only; the Friday train did not run after 1960. The route is still used on summer Saturdays and Sundays by a train from Oxford.

In the 1950s most of the WR trains were powered by Hall class 4-6-0s from Weymouth or Westbury sheds. Granges were seen to a lesser extent. The heaviest types, the King and 47XX classes, were not permitted on the route, but Castles were not uncommon. In 1952/3 No 4080 *Powderham Castle* frequently worked the 12.30 Paddington–Weymouth; the return working was the 18.35 milk train. A Bath Road Castle sometimes worked the 08.05 Bristol–Weymouth and 12.35 return. The summer Channel Islands Boat Express

WR 0-4-2T No 1433 shunts a lengthy empty stock train at Weymouth on June 8, 1959. [S. Rickard

Ivatt Class 2 2-6-2T No 41320 stops at Upwey & Broadwey with a Bournemouth—Weymouth train on September 17, 1966. [D. H. Cape

Standard Class 4 2-6-0 No 76057 and Battle of Britain 4-6-2 No 34077 storm up the 1 in 50 from Weymouth towards Dorchester with a Waterloo train on April 19, 1965. [D. H. Cape

was normally handled by an Old Oak Common Castle.

In June 1959 most of the regular workings were taken over by diesel multiple-units. Locomotive-hauled trains were wholly steam-worked until 1962, when Hymek diesels began a gradual takeover.

The Channel Islands perishable trains, mainly carrying tomatoes, are a feature of the summer months. In the 1950s nearly all of them used the WR route to reach the Midlands, South Wales, or the North. They were worked by Halls, 43XX 2-6-0s or 28XX 2-8-0s. In the summer of 1960 seven perishable trains were scheduled to leave Weymouth each weekday. The following year there were five, mainly in the hands of Weymouth's Standard Class 5 4-6-0s. By 1965 Hymek diesels had taken over.

In the 1950s a local service ran on the WR about every one or two hours. Trains ran from Weymouth to Yeovil (Pen Mill), Maiden Newton or Dorchester West. Some ran to and from Yeovil Town by reversing at Pen Mill. They generally consisted of either a 14XX 0-4-2T working push-and-pull, or the WR diesel railcar which was based at Weymouth. These trains served two halts at Monkton & Came and Upwey Wishing Well, between Dorchester and Upwey which were closed in January 1957; they were never served by any of the Southern trains.

After 1959 the Castle Cary–Weymouth line declined steadily. In 1963 the Beeching Report recommended that all intermediate traffic over the Bristol–Weymouth route should be discontinued, including the closure of Yeovil (Pen Mill), Maiden Newton and Dorchester West stations. This was not accepted in full, but in October 1966 seven stations and halts between Westbury and Dorchester were closed. Already a year earlier the Sunday service over the line in winter had been reduced to one train in each direction, and has remained so ever since.

By the middle of 1966 all remaining freight traffic on the WR line had been diverted to the SR to reach Westbury via Eastleigh and Salisbury, but the seasonal tomato trains were an exception and used the Castle Cary route until it was singled in 1968. From then on these trains were diverted via Basingstoke and Southcote Junction.

Regular services on the Southern line

The Weymouth line has always been one of the main lines from Waterloo, since the LSWR first reached the town. The original main line ran via Ringwood, Wimborne and Broadstone; the present route via Bournemouth was not opened until 1893. A local service ran over the old route between Bournemouth and Brockenhurst until that line was closed in May 1964; until 1963 it had been used each summer by two or three Saturday trains between Waterloo and Weymouth or Swanage, which left the normal route at Lymington Junction and rejoined it at Hamworthy Junction.

In the mid 1950s express trains ran between Waterloo and Weymouth about every two hours, leaving Waterloo on the half-hour, and Weymouth at approximately the same time. Only a small portion of the train normally ran right through to Weymouth; the main part was detached at Bournemouth Central, and terminated at Bournemouth West until that station was closed in September 1965. In nearly all cases, however, the main line engine worked through to Weymouth.

Leaving Bournemouth Central, the Weymouth train passes the remnants of the Bournemouth West triangle. The line to Bournemouth West left the main line at Gas Works Junction and crossed a viaduct before the steep descent into the West station. Bournemouth West carriage sidings are still in use; access is via the west side of the triangle to the main line at Branksome. Beyond Branksome is the steep descent, mainly at 1 in 60, of Parkstone bank, by which the line reaches sea level and curves sharply into Poole. West of Poole, at Holes Bay Junction, what is left of the Somerset & Dorset line turns off to the right; the main line crosses Poole Harbour on a long causeway built in 1893, and soon joins the old route at Hamworthy Junction. The first few hundred yards of the old route and of the old Hamworthy branch are still used as carriage sidings.

The next place of importance is Wareham, junction for Swanage. Until September 1962 three Weymouth expresses in each direction carried through coaches for Swanage; they were then discontinued, but reintroduced to the extent of one train per day after the Bournemouth electrification. Full length trains ran to Swanage on summer Saturdays, mainly via the old route. The Swanage branch leaves the main line one mile west of Wareham at Worgret Junction.

The next station is Wool, which has become more important since the building of Winfrith atomic station, and now almost all trains call there. The train continues on a steadily rising gradient through Moreton to Dorchester South.

In the mid 1950s the best trains covered the journey from Waterloo to Weymouth in 3¼ hours. In June 1957 two-hour schedules were reintroduced between Waterloo and Bournemouth for the first time for some ten years, and on a wider scale than previously; the 10.30 Waterloo then reached Weymouth in exactly 3 hr, and the 18.30 in 3 hr 4 min. The fastest up train was the 17.35 from Weymouth, with a time of 3 hr 5 min. Bournemouth two-hour schedules with steam power lasted until June 1965, when there was a general deceleration on account of the electrification works.

In 1951 the line received its first named train, in honour of the Festival of Britain. This was the "Royal Wessex", which lasted until July 1967. It was by no means the fastest train on the line; it departed Waterloo at 16.35 and Weymouth at 07.34 and also carried portions for Swanage and Bournemouth West.

In addition there was the overnight mail train in each direction, although no sleeping cars were conveyed. Up and down trains began their journeys at about 22.15 or 22.30, and, after reversing at Southampton Terminus, reached their destinations some five hours later.

In the 1950s SR local trains mostly ran to and from Bournemouth Central. In the 1957 summer service one or two served unusual places; there was a 06.40 from Weymouth to Brockenhurst via Broadstone and Ringwood; a 14.20 to Andover Junction via Eastleigh and Romsey; and a 19.48 to Reading General via Basingstoke. In the down direction there was a 03.25 from Salisbury via the single-track Fordingbridge line. This was a passenger and newspaper train, and connected with the Waterloo to West of England newspaper train at Salisbury. There was no direct Waterloo–Weymouth newspaper train until summer 1964, after the closure of the Fordingbridge line.

In the 1950s the Waterloo expresses were worked mainly by Bulleid Pacifics from Nine Elms or Bournemouth sheds. Most trains were hauled by the same engine throughout. Weymouth shed took over the Nine Elms Merchant Navy turns in 1964.

Most local trains in the 1950s were worked by Bournemouth or Eastleigh King Arthurs, with an occasional Lord Nelson or H15. In the 1960s they were gradually taken over by Weymouth's standard Class 5 4-6-0s, and standard 2-6-0s from Bournemouth or Eastleigh. In 1963 Hampshire diesel units began working most of the local trains on summer Saturdays, and continued to do so until the Bournemouth electrification, but they never penetrated as far as Weymouth at any other time.

Class 33 Sulzer diesels first came to the SR Western Section in 1962; although they now handle practically the entire service between Bournemouth and Weymouth, they were hardly seen as far west as Weymouth until summer 1966. They could then work passenger trains only in summer, for they were not equipped for steam heating. The first diesels to reach Weymouth were Nos 10201 and 10202, which began working some Waterloo–Weymouth turns early in 1952. When working they usually did two round trips per day. The following year they were joined on the SR by Nos 10000 and 10001 from the LMR, which worked frequently between Waterloo and Weymouth in 1953 and 1954. Towards the end of 1954 all these diesels were transferred to the LMR.

In October 1966 Brush/Sulzer Class 47 diesels began working on the Waterloo–Weymouth line, after three of this type had been allocated to Eastleigh. From July 10, 1967, nearly all Bournemouth–Weymouth services have been formed from through trains from Waterloo. The Weymouth portion consists of one, or at busy periods two, four-car trailer 4TC units, which are propelled from London to Bournemouth by a 4 REP electric unit. At Bournemouth a push-pull fitted Class 33 diesel simply backs on to the front of the Weymouth portion. For up trains the procedure is exactly the reverse: the trailer unit is propelled from Weymouth to Bournemouth by the Class 33 diesel and attached to the rear of a 4REP unit and another trailer unit.

Waterloo–Weymouth trains are now either fast or semi-fast. Fast trains leave Waterloo at 30 min past even hours, and Weymouth at 35 min past odd hours. The fastest times introduced by the July 1967 timetable were four down trains covering the journey in 2 hr 41 min, and five up trains in 2 hr 45 min, the time between London and Bournemouth being a standard 100 min. A feature of the timetable is that the fast timings apply to Sundays as as well as weekdays. The semi-fast trains to Weymouth leave Waterloo at 47 min past even hours, and Weymouth at 42 min past even hours; they become stopping trains between Bournemouth and Weymouth, and complete the journey in about 3 hr 20 min. These services are in fact hourly between Waterloo and Bournemouth. In July 1967 it became possible to leave Weymouth on a weekday morning and be in London at 09.24.

Boat trains

The Channel Islands ships came under the Southern Region in 1950 but the boat trains continued to run from Paddington until November 1959. In the summer months the Paddington boat train, running each weekday, was the most important train to pass through Dorchester. It was a full-length train, one of the few not calling at Dorchester West, and was usually worked by an Old Oak Common Castle, or sometimes a Modified Hall. The same engine worked both down and up trains; the train left Paddington at 08.20, and returned from Weymouth Quay at 15.45.

A curious procedure took place at Weymouth Junction. The train carried a restaurant car, but it was not taken on to the quay. The car was always the second coach of the train; when engines were changed at Weymouth Junction, the main line engine removed the front two coaches. A 1366 class 0-6-0PT backed on, and drew the remainder of the train on to the Quay tramway. The two coaches were restored to the up train at Weymouth Junction in the afternoon.

On summer Saturdays the down train ran in two parts. The first part left Paddington at 08.20 and was advertised non-stop to Weymouth Quay, although taking exactly the same time on the journey as the weekday train with three stops. In fact, the Saturday 08.20 made four working stops: at Heywood Road Junction to change enginemen; at Yetminster to attach a banker as far as Evershot; at Weymouth Junction to take on a conductor; and on the Portland branch to change engines. Summer Saturdays were too busy to allow engine changing on the main line. This train included a restaurant car which did make the journey on to the Quay, and so was marshalled in the middle. The 08.20 was usually a 12 coach train worked by a Reading Hall.

The main train left Paddington at 08.30 on Saturdays. It called at Reading to take up only, and made no more advertised calls to Weymouth Quay, although making the same working stops as the 08.20. The 08.30 was almost invariably Castle-hauled, and although its booked load was 11 coaches, up to 1957 it often loaded to 14. As on weekdays the front two coaches were detached before going on to the Quay.

In the summer there were additional sailings each way on Saturday nights, although the outward sailing operated only at peak week-ends. The inward boat train, leaving Weymouth Quay for Paddington in the early hours of Sunday morning, was duplicated in July and August.

Another boat train connected with the mid-day sailing on summer Saturdays. This was the 08.00 Birmingham (Snow Hill), usually worked by a Hall from Tyseley shed. The train conveyed two portions, the front for Weymouth Town, the rear for Weymouth Quay, detached at Weymouth Junction. In 1960 it was replaced by a 07.15 from Birmingham, but after two summers the Weymouth Quay portion of this train was withdrawn, and passengers were taken on by bus.

A more complicated arrangement took place in the up direction on summer Saturday afternoons. A train left Weymouth Quay at 16.05 for Cardiff and Birmingham; at Weymouth Junction it was attached to the rear of the 16.18 Weymouth Town–Cardiff, so that the two Cardiff portions were next to each other. The train divided again into Cardiff and Birmingham portions at Westbury. This arrangement remained unaltered until the end of summer 1964.

In winter there were three Channel Islands sailings each week, outward by night, inward by day. In 1949 a boat train left Paddington at 21.10, and the return train ran to the same timing as in summer. After that year the independent boat trains were withdrawn in winter, and Quay portions were attached to the rear of regular services. The Quay portion travelled down with the 18.00 from Paddington, and went up attached to the 16.10 Weymouth–Paddington; on sailing days this train left Weymouth Town five minutes earlier to allow for the attachment of the portion at Weymouth Junction.

On November 2, 1959, the Channel Islands Boat trains were transferred from Paddington to Waterloo. In winter the boat sailed as before outwards by night and back by day. Winter boat trains were at first restored, and left Waterloo at 21.15 and Weymouth Quay at 15.45, running non-stop between Poole and Weymouth. Sailings were reduced to twice a week in midwinter, from November to February, but operated three times a week in spring and autumn.

In the winter of 1962–3 the up boat train was withdrawn altogether, and passengers were taken by bus to catch the 15.50 Weymouth Town–Waterloo. The 21.15 down boat train was still advertised, but in practice was often combined with the 21.20 Waterloo–Poole in the winter months.

The winter service was practically unchanged by the Bournemouth electrification in 1967. In the down direction the 21.47 Waterloo–Bournemouth semi-fast carried a portion for Weymouth Quay twice a week, but through coaches in winter were withdrawn after two years. The 20.30 Waterloo–Weymouth express is met by buses for the Quay, and returning passengers are taken by bus to the Town station to catch the 15.35 Waterloo express.

In summer 1960 the day boat train left Waterloo at 08.27 and returned from Weymouth Quay at 15.45, an out-and-home turn for a Nine Elms light Pacific. The journey time was almost the same as from Paddington. On Friday nights from mid-July to the end of August there was an additional crossing in each direction: the down boat train left Waterloo at 19.45 on Friday evenings and the up train left Weymouth Quay at 05.55 on Saturdays, arriving at Waterloo at 09.33. On summer Saturdays an 08.02 from Waterloo ran as a relief to the 08.27. It called only at Southampton Central and ran via Ringwood. All these trains were generally in the hands of Nine Elms Light Pacifics.

The most important development took place in May 1961. Until that time there had been regular crossings to the Channel Islands by the longer sea route from Southampton. The Southampton steamers were old; about the same time two new vessels, the *Caesarea* and *Sarnia*, began service on the Weymouth route. In May 1961 all the Southampton–Channel Islands services were transferred to

RIGHT: Another view of Upwey Wishing Well Halt, this time with Standard Class 5 4-6-0 No 73018 piloting West Country Pacific No 34047 *Callington* with the 17.20 Weymouth—Waterloo on Easter Monday, 1967. [John H. Bird

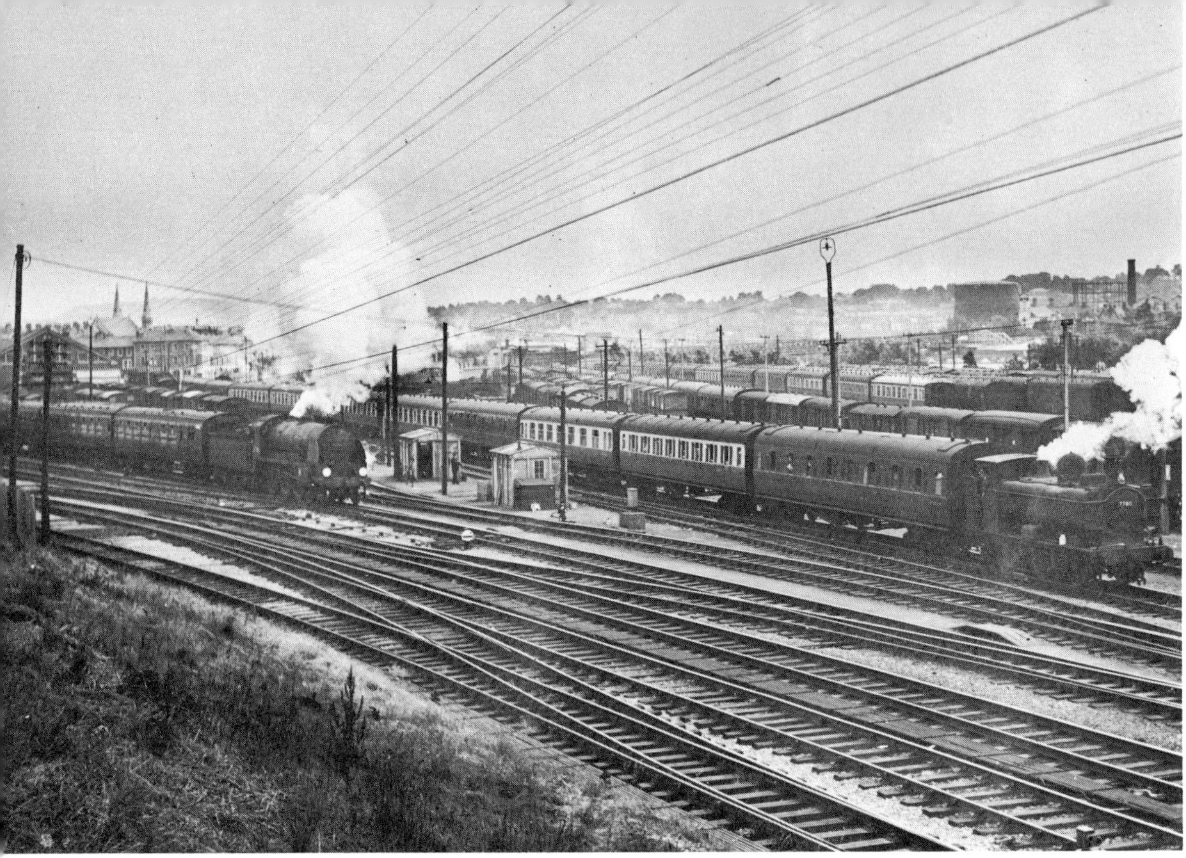

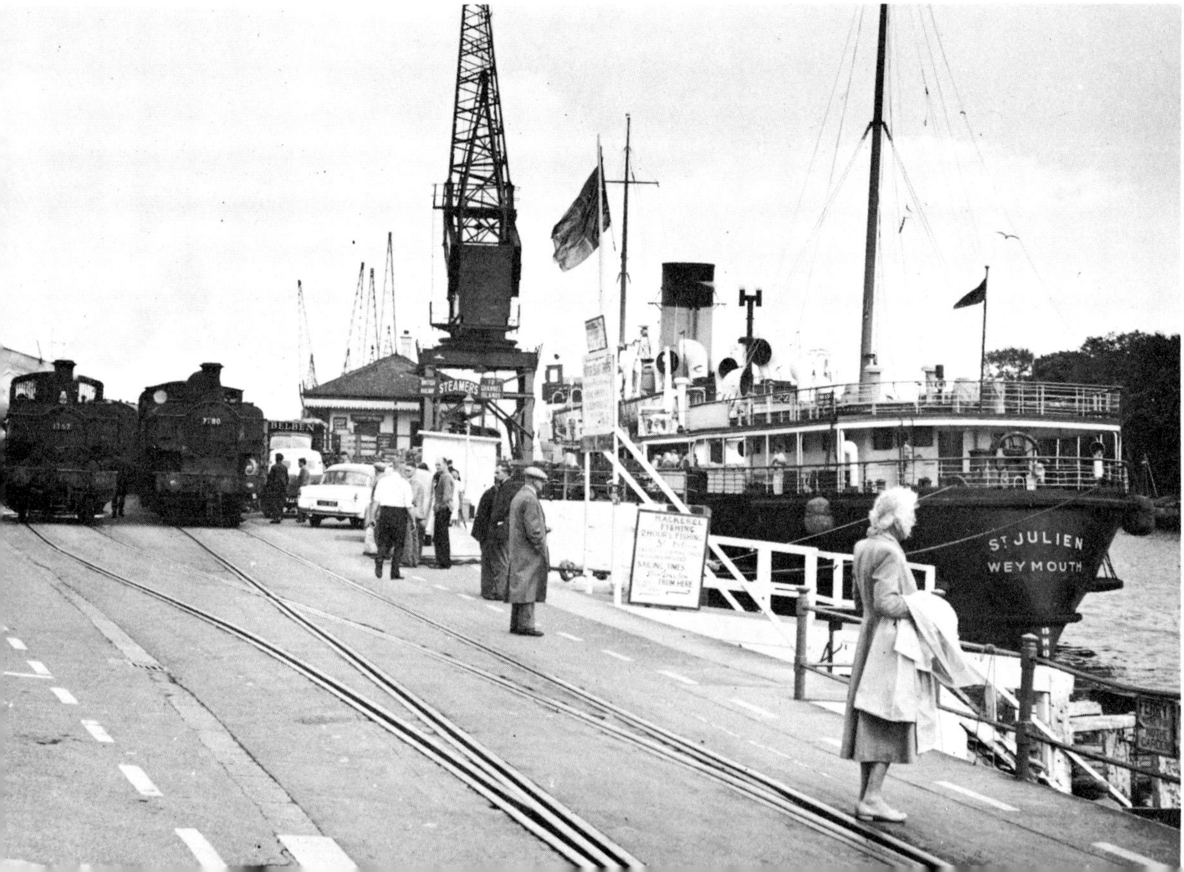
STEAMERS
BELBEN
MACKEREL
FISHING
SAILING TIMES
FROM HERE
ST JULIEN
WEYMOUTH

LEFT: WR 0-6-0PT No 7780 comes to a stand with the Weymouth Quay—Paddington Boat Train as King Arthur Class 4-6-0 No 30786 leaves with the 15.50 Weymouth—Bournemouth stopping train on June 12, 1959. [S. Rickard

Weymouth. That summer the times of the daily boat trains were altered to 08.10 down and 16.00 up, and remained the same until July 1967. On Friday and Saturday nights in summer there were two outward and one inward crossings. The Saturday boat trains for the day crossing left Waterloo at 07.58 (unadvertised) and 08.15. The 07.58 ran via Ringwood for three summers until the closure of that line in May 1964.

In the inward direction two Channel Islands boats arrived at Weymouth at 14.15 and 15.30 on summer Saturday afternoons from 1961 to 1963, connecting with a total of four boat trains which left Weymouth Quay at 14.45 (via Ringwood), 15.00, 16.00 and 16.30. Only the 15.00 and 16.30 were advertised. Five Nine Elms West Country Pacifics were rostered to handle the various boat trains on 1963 summer Saturdays:

Duty No.	*Outward*	*Inward*
37	1. Friday night	2. 05.55 Weymouth Quay
	3. 12.35 Waterloo–Weymouth	4. Sunday morning
39	08.15 Waterloo–Weymouth Quay	16.30 Weymouth Quay
40	09.25 Wimbledon–Weymouth	16.00 Weymouth Quay
41	07.45 Waterloo–Weymouth	15.00 Weymouth Quay
46	07.57 Waterloo–Weymouth Quay	14.45 Weymouth Quay

In 1964 there began a fortnightly overnight crossing to St Malo during the summer months, with connecting boat trains in each direction running to the same times as the Channel Islands Boat trains. The sea crossing from Weymouth was 2–3 hours shorter than from Southampton. The following summer the service operated once a week, but after that the railway-operated steamers to St Malo from both Southampton and Weymouth were withdrawn.

LEFT: Weymouth Quay on June 9, 1959 with 0-6-0PTs Nos 1367 and 7780 waiting to work boat trains to Weymouth Town. [S. Rickard

The summer day-time boat trains retained steam-haulage up to July 7, 1967. From July 10, Class 47 diesels took over the regular boat trains, and Class 47s and 33s worked the summer Saturday trains. The trains were accelerated by 30–40 min to reach Weymouth Quay in approximately 3 hr.

The following summer the outward sailing was retarded by one hour, and the down boat train was retimed to leave Waterloo at 09.55. The Class 47 diesels were replaced by Class 74 electro-diesel locomotives, which meant that the trains had to change to Class 33 haulage at Bournemouth, since the diesel engine of the Class 74 did not give sufficient power to haul trains at speed over the non-electrified section.

Holiday traffic

During the nineteen-fifties there was, on the Weymouth line as on all coastal routes, an immense concentration of holiday traffic on Saturdays from mid-June to mid-September, and the scene on such days was unrecognisable from the ordinary weekday service. The intensity of summer Saturday traffic reached a peak between 1956 and 1958; since then there has been a gradual decline, although ten years later on most lines summer Saturdays are still busier than any other day. But excursions ran on other summer weekdays, for example the 09.05 Salisbury to Weymouth and 18.20 back via Fordingbridge on Mondays to Fridays from mid-July to the end of August.

Another ran on Mondays to Thursdays from mid-July to the end of August, the 10.55 Yeovil (Pen Mill)–Weymouth. It ran non-stop, and was invariably hauled by one of Weymouth shed's Class 51XX tanks, No 4133 or 4166, running bunker-first. There was no return working.

A long-standing Sunday excursion was the 09.33 Waterloo-Bournemouth, which ran all the year round until July 1967. On alternate Sundays in the summer months it was extended to Weymouth, returning from there at 18.40; in 1957 for example, it called at Surbiton and Woking, and then ran non-stop to Bournemouth Central. Since July 1967 there have been no regular advertised excursion trains, but excursion fares are available to Bournemouth and Weymouth by all services leaving Waterloo before mid-day on a Sunday.

Two regular Sunday excursions ran down the WR line to Weymouth in summer during the nineteen-fifties. These were the 09.40 Parson Street, which ran non-stop from Bath Spa to Weymouth, and the 10.0 Swindon, which was non-stop from Frome. They returned from Weymouth at 19.20 and 20.30 respectively. In the summer of 1970 a train ran from Oxford to Weymouth and back on Sundays via the former Wilts, Somerset & Weymouth line from Chippenham. There was also a Sunday 09.10 from Bristol running non-stop between Bath and Yeovil.

On summer Saturdays in the 1950s trains left Waterloo for Weymouth about every hour from 07.30 to 16.30. The morning departures were mainly full-length trains of up to twelve coaches all destined for Weymouth, the heaviest being the 10.30, and most conveyed restaurant cars. The 07.30 Waterloo ran via Ringwood. The 08.32 (advertised departure 08.30) had the tightest timing to Weymouth, 3 hr 14 min in 1957, but frequently arrived up to ½ hr late. Like other full-length trains, it was not allowed sufficient time for the difficult section between Bournemouth Central and Weymouth, with three or four intermediate stops, and often needed to draw up twice at the short platforms. Also when a path was used for an 08.28 Waterloo–Southampton Docks boat train, the 8.32 could be seriously delayed before Southampton. From 1959 onwards it was allowed an extra 14 min of overall journey time.

The 07.30, 08.32 and 10.30 were usually hauled by Light Pacifics; the 09.24, 11.22 and 12.35 usually by Lord Nelsons or King Arthurs or, later, Class 5 4–6–0s.

The down Waterloo trains did not call at many intermediate stations on Saturdays for they were catered for by the 09.25 Wimbledon –Weymouth semi-fast. This train used the local line all the way to Worting Junction, and was usually hauled by a King Arthur or H15.

The regular up Waterloo expresses, which on weekdays conveyed portions from Bournemouth West and sometimes Swanage, were divided on Saturdays, so that, except for the 07.34 "Royal Wessex", all the Weymouth portions ran as separate trains, usually conveying restaurant cars.

Another feature of the summer Saturday service was that certain Weymouth–Bournemouth stopping trains were extended to Waterloo. The 08.25 Weymouth called at all stations to Bournemouth Central, including Radipole Halt, and then suddenly ran the 108 miles on to Waterloo without further stops, even at Southampton. The 12.20 Weymouth was extended from Bournemouth in the same way, except that it did make further stops, including Woking, Surbiton and Wimbledon to set down only. The 10.10 Weymouth–Bournemouth Central was extended to Waterloo on Saturdays for the first time in summer 1955, in the timings of a former Bournemouth West–Woking stopping train. This gave a through Weymouth–Waterloo train which called at virtually every station as far as Woking, and completed the journey in 5 hr 32 min.

One of the most interesting Saturday up trains was the 11.02 Weymouth–Waterloo. This was a five coach train which at Wareham became the rear portion of the 11.34 Swanage. The Weymouth portion, usually worked by a Q class 0-6-0, reached Wareham first. The engine then ran round its train and pulled the coaches on to the down line, west of the station. The heavier Swanage portion came up behind a Light Pacific, and the Weymouth portion was shunted on behind. The combined train of 13 coaches used the Ringwood route, and made only one more stop, at Southampton, before reaching Waterloo five minutes ahead of the 11.25 Weymouth. This arrangement (which lasted until the end of summer 1966) often blocked up and down lines at Wareham for as much as 20 min.

The restaurant cars for the early Saturday departures from Weymouth came down, unadvertised, on some of the regular Friday afternoon and evening expresses, instead of forming part of the Bournemouth West portions.

The most memorable feature of those summer Saturdays, to an observer at Dorchester, was the mid-day procession of down expresses from the WR. These six trains were often referred to collectively as the "boat trains", although only three were wholly or partly for the Channel Islands. They were scheduled to pass Dorchester Junction between about 11.30 and 12.30; in practice they often did not begin to appear until after 12 noon, or finish passing until well after one o'clock. Four of them were Saturdays only trains, and all but one passed non-stop through Dorchester West.

The first was the 09.10 (SO) from Bristol, a heavy train often hauled by a 43XX class Mogul of St Philip's Marsh shed; it called at Bath Spa, Frome, Yeovil, Maiden Newton and Dorchester West, and its running could affect the whole of the series. The 08.32 Waterloo was supposed to be next past Dorchester Junction; then came the 08.20 and 08.30 Paddington–Weymouth Quay. The next was the 09.43 Bristol, which actually ran through from Weston-Super-Mare, and was a version of the regular 09.25 Bristol with some of its stops cut out; the 09.43 called at Bradford-on-Avon, Trowbridge, Westbury, Castle Cary and Yeovil, and was headed usually by a Westbury or Weymouth Hall. The last two trains were the 07.50 and 08.00 from Birmingham (Snow Hill), usually worked by Halls or Granges from Tyseley shed, although sometimes bringing a County class 4-6-0 into the area. The 08.00 with its two portions has already been described; it called at Leamington Spa, Oxford, Swindon and Yeovil (to set down only). The 07.50 was first advertised as a relief to the 08.00 in 1951 or 1952, and in the whole of its journey made only one passenger stop at Swindon.

The Bristol and Birmingham trains converged at Bradford Junction, and this flow converged with the Paddington trains at Fairwood Junction, Westbury. The first obstacle confronting the procession on the Weymouth line was the Evershot bank. All except the 09.43 Bristol, an eight coach train, stopped at Yetminster to take on a banker as far as Evershot; until 1958 this was not made very clear in the WR working timetable, some trains being allowed 4 min for banking purposes, one 10 min, and others not shown as allowed any time. Until the enlargement of the arrival side at Weymouth Town in 1956/7, considerable congestion used to build up between Dorchester and Weymouth. One Saturday in August 1955 almost every train in this group was stopped for several minutes at Dorchester Junction starting signal

Three trains left Weymouth for the Midlands on summer Saturday mornings and in summer 1958 a Saturday 06.00 Cardiff–Weymouth began running, which returned at 13.35. This was steam-hauled for the first year, but in 1959 it became a nine-coach train of diesel multiple-unit stock.

From 1959 onwards WR summer Saturday traffic decreased, the main change being the rerouting of the Channel Islands boat trains to Waterloo in 1959/60, and the subsequent decline of the WR route. There was no radical alteration of the SR service until July 1967, although it was gradually reduced during the early 1960s; the 09.25 Wimbledon–Weymouth was withdrawn after 1963, the morning Weymouth–Bournemouth stopping trains no longer ran through to Waterloo after 1961, and the afternoon up expresses ceased to run separately from the Bournemouth West portions. In 1963 Hampshire diesel units began working through to Weymouth on some local services from Eastleigh; 1963 was also the last summer in which any trains ran via Ringwood to avoid Bournemouth.

In the early 1960s the 20 or so Standard 5MT 4-6-0s allocated to Nine Elms completed their take-over from the Lord Nelson, King

Arthur and Schools classes; and by 1963 the only main line passenger steam locomotives on the line were the Standards and the Bulleid Pacifics. Nevertheless until the end of 1962, even Schools class 4-4-0s sometimes worked Weymouth expresses from Waterloo on summer Saturdays.

Since 1967 the regular weekday service between Waterloo and Weymouth has run unchanged on summer Saturdays, except that most of the fast trains carry an 8-coach portion for Weymouth and some are double-headed west of Bournemouth. At first there were only three additional Saturday trains, two down and one up, and in 1969 this was reduced to one in each direction. In summer 1970, however, after all through coach workings between the main line and the Swanage branch had been withdrawn, three extra Saturday trains have run in each direction between Waterloo and Weymouth. Some of these are former Waterloo–Swanage expresses diverted to Weymouth, most are diesel-hauled throughout, and one, the 10.05 up, does not call at Bournemouth.

Despite the gradual run-down of the cross country trains between Weymouth and the Midlands, 1965 saw the introduction of a new summer Saturday cross-country buffet car express, the 06.10 Derby–Weymouth and 12.45 return, serving Birmingham (New Street) and Bristol. The southbound train is a combination of two separate regular trains running from Derby to Bristol and Bristol to Weymouth; at Weymouth it connects with buses for the Quay. A Peak Class 45 diesel hauls the train from Derby to Bristol (Temple Meads), where the train reverses.

After the closure of Bournemouth West station in September 1965, most of the Bournemouth cross-country trains began running to and from Poole, and some ran as empty stock between Poole and Weymouth. For example, in 1967 a Warship left Weymouth with empty stock at 12.05 on summer Saturdays, and ran non-stop to Poole, where it formed the 13.12 to Swansea via Eastleigh. In summer 1968 this operating procedure was made public, and through Saturday services were announced between Weymouth and Liverpool via Bournemouth and Basingstoke, and Weymouth and Cardiff via Bournemouth and Eastleigh. The Cardiff train departs Cardiff at 10.00 and Weymouth at 12.22, and takes just over 5 hr compared with the 4 hr of the trains using the more direct WR route. The Liverpool train was diverted to Manchester in summer 1970 and re-routed via Willesden. It leaves Weymouth at 08.25 and Manchester at 10.32, and has a journey time of just under 7 hr. A Class 33 diesel works the train, which travels up the Waterloo main line as far as Byfleet Junction, then via Virginia Water, Twickenham, Clapham Junction and Kensington (Olympia) to Willesden. An LMR electric locomotive takes over at Willesden.

In 20 years at Weymouth not only have the multitude of WR and SR steam classes given way to more standardised diesel types, but virtually the whole pattern of operation has changed. It may change again if the third rail is extended west from Bournemouth.

LEFT: Castle Class 4-6-0 No 7020 and WR 2-6-0 No 5370 leave Weymouth with the boat train to Paddington depicted earlier, on June 12, 1959.
[S. Rickard

Something for the workers

R. L. GWILLAM

ABOVE: In its last years the Highworth branch staff train from Swindon was diesel worked with a shunting locomotive; No D2195 heads the evening working to Highworth near Hannington on June 18, 1962.
[D. H. Ballantyne

THE MEN and women who worked "inside"—(not, as may be inferred from this expression, in the "nick", but those who were employed in the Swindon Works of the former Great Western Railway Company, latterly British Railways, Western Region), were conveyed between their home stations and Swindon Junction station, morning and evening, by what were generally conceded to be special trains. In only one case was this so, the remainder being available for use by the general public. The exception was the Highworth branch train, which operated over a line otherwise closed to passenger traffic.

There were six such special trains, morning and evening; reading clockwise, as it were, round the compass, they ran from and to Cirencester (Watermoor); Highworth; Shrivenham; Chiseldon; Wootton Bassett; and Purton. The Purton evening train was extended to Kemble, where it connected with branch services for Tetbury and Cirencester (Town), and also with a "car" which came up from Chalford. Later, this was altered, and the connection was with the erstwhile substitute for the old "Cheltenham Flyer", for Gloucester.

The workings of the various trains at the time I knew them in the post war years made interesting reading—and, in some cases, had a touch of humour, as will be told. Very little in the workings of engines and stock was wasted. The enginemen were drawn from No 8 Link (known as the Old Town Link), and this was one step up from the Pilot Link, and one below the general Goods Link, which itself was the Control Link, since, at that time, all workings were under the jurisdiction of the Control. Taking the workings in sequence, and from the morning runs, the Watermoor engine was off shed at around 05.15, and ran light to Swindon Town, where it picked up coaches already standing on the back road. Officially a passenger train, in all the time I worked this Link, I never saw a single person, other than railwaymen, use it. Traffic on the "Tiddley Dike" the MSWJ, at that hour of the day, was very sparse! At Watermoor, the engine ran round the train, topped up with water, and was right away at 06.40, calling at South Cerney and Cricklade before a storming finish up Old Town bank. Here, the men were decanted, and crossed the platform to the Chiseldon train, which had arrived only seconds previously. The two minutes allowed at Old Town was rigidly observed, since a smart run to Swindon Junction was necessary if the men were to arrive in time to walk from the station to their clocking-in places in the Works by the last hooter.

The engine of the Watermoor then went to Old Town yard as pilot for the rest of the morning, which involved banking trains up from Rushey Platt, fetching horse boxes from the Transfer for Marlborough and any other job considered necessary. The stock was picked up by a 45XX engine from Swindon, and formed the branch stock on the Marlborough –Savernake service.

Highworth engine: off shed at about 06.00, and light to Swindon Junction Station, where the stock for the branch was kept in the bay known as The Shed. This name was a reminder of when the locomotive shed was part of Swindon station, up end. After the trip, the stock went to local work, usually on Didcot line stoppers, while the engine went as works pilot on the Carriage side, shunting between the Milk Bank and the Bristol line carriage works. The engine was always a 14XX class, and, when I fired it, I found it an arduous task, for the final haul to Highworth is up a steep and curving bank, making it necessary to have a box of fire at the Hannington end, and standing with the engine ramping its head off all the while we stood at Highworth after running round the train. This station possessed what I believe to be the oldest working dummy (ground signal) on the Western—a real museum piece, if ever I saw one. I wonder what happened to it?

The Shrivenham train engine went off shed at about 05.45, picked up its stock from the Water Sidings (alongside the Gloucester Up side platform), ran non-stop to Shrivenham, where, after crossing over, the usual two minutes was allowed for loading before the right away. The engine ran round the train on the up side, utilising the goods shed road and a spur to the stop-blocks. I remember the driver telling me, on my first trip on this train (and, incidentally, my first trip east of the Transfer) as we approached Bourton bridge that this was the spot where a King on the Plymouth-Paddington sleeper came off the road and nearly demolished the bridge, being so badly damaged in the process that she was almost scrapped, but that pride and determination not to admit to the public that the accident was really as bad as all that caused a re-think, and the saving, at heavy cost, of the engine.

Calling at Stratton Park Halt, the Shrivenham workmen's train was a flyer to Swindon, vieing with the Bassett and the Purton for the privilege of being first in. These main line trains brought keen rivalry on punctual, and preferably ultra-punctual, arrivals. Speeds of the order of 60 and 70 mph were not uncommon. Raise the eyebrows, if you will, but these are facts. I believe I am right in saying that some of these works trains were booked

Highworth in steam days with 0-4-2T No 5804 running round the branch train after arrival from Swindon on September 6, 1952. [H. C. Casserley

Another view of the Highworth branch train, this time leaving Swindon on July 4, 1947 behind 0-4-2T No 5800. [H. C. Casserley

The west end of Swindon station with Warship Type 4 No D829 about to leave with the 12.30 Paddington — Weston-super-Mare. The bay platforms on the right hand side were often used by the workmen's trains described by the author. [J. A. Fleming

at 60 mph, start-to-stop, over these short (6 mile maximum) hauls. On arrival at Swindon, and having dislodged the passengers, the engine retired to Water sidings, and there acted as pilot for the morning; the stock went to local work on the Bristol line.

The Wootton Bassett train was also a star turn: a runner from the word "go". Off shed at 06.00, it took the stock from the main down-line siding at Whitehouse Bridge, and shot off to Bassett at a rapid rate. Running on, it stood in the down side yard for a quarter of an hour, usually, then crossed over, having run round in the long loop. Once the right-away was given, the sparks flew. We used to think that the men enjoyed the friendly rivalry which existed between the Purton train and the Bassett train. The Bassett run had the disadvantage of an uphill start, whereas the Purton enjoyed a downhill run all the way. It was compensated for in some degree by the difference in starting times, the Bassett train pinching a minute start whenever possible—but it was not known if the Purton train did not do the same! The rivalry between the trains had a practical edge to it—the train to arrive first simply cut-off, and left the coaches at the platform and so had a few minutes extra breakfast time; the second arrival had to put the coaches of both trains away, involving crossing over the main line, since one set was required on the down side. The engine of the Bassett train was then station pilot for the morning, while the Purton engine was right away to shed again; this job was a sinecure for the Union Branch secretary, giving him the time to do his union work, while being available on the shed for locomotive duties (or should it be the other way round?). It was, I suppose, inevitable that the Purton train should be first in, most mornings.

The Purton engine was off shed at about 06.00—there was quite a bunch at the shed starter round this time of the morning, what with pilots for the works, train engines and what-have-you; I suppose that 06.00 was about the busiest time of the day for engines off shed.

There remains the Chiseldon train. This engine was first to leave the shed—around 05.00, or it may have been a quarter of an hour earlier. It worked the first goods of the day up to Old Town, a train usually requiring two engines. Guaranteed a clear road through Rushey Platt, they made a brave sight especially on clear, still, autumn mornings, just getting light, with the smoke from the two pannier tanks making great columns in the air, marching with the engines, and marking their usually-slow progress up the bank to Old Town. In the yard, the Chiseldon engine cut off, picked up the coaches which had formed the last train from the Savernake–Marlborough branch the previous day and ran smartly to Chiseldon, running round the train, and being right away as soon as it was coupled up, the passengers loading while the engine ran round—the only instance among all the works trains. After unloading at Swindon Junction, the engine then went to the Transfer, and proceeded to change with the engine of each yard in turn. There are (or were) four of these, two on the up side, and two on the down, which meant that four pilots had to be changed, taken to shed, the fires cleaned, and coal and water taken on, before returning to the next yard. This, not unnaturally, occupied the crew for the best part of their working day; also not unnaturally it was the least liked of all the turns in this link.

The evening trains were reversals of the morning trains, except for the Purton, which I mentioned earlier. Engines and stock were at the end of their working day, for the most part, again with the exception of the Purton, which had exchanged the 64XX 0-6-0 PT for a 45XX engine, and which continued in service until 22.00 (last train from Kemble), working the Kemble line locals. The majority of the stock was put into the sidings for cleaning and re-marshalling during the night. The engines went to shed for servicing, and were made ready for the morning turns, each engine for these trains being stabled in a time-honoured stand on shed—some round the small table, some on the straight roads, and a couple in the big shed. The crews allocated to these works trains knew exactly where to go for their engines—no reference needing to be made to the stabling list which gave engine numbers and where they were to be found when booking-on.

The only train on which I did not work was the Purton morning; all the others fell to my lot while I was in No 8 Link, and the turns usually came round about every two or three months. I managed to dodge a lot of them, by exchanging turns with Control Link men, who, for various (usually female) reasons, wanted an early turn when they were on a late run. In this way, being a willing hand, I had a fair amount of main line running instead of pilot work. I also became more experienced with the larger classes of engines more quickly than I would had I stuck to my proper link working. Whether it did me any good is doubtful, since I left the footplate before I got into the passenger links. Even so, I had a fair whack of passenger working, on the same route as when I was in the Old Town Link by exchanging turns! This latter has nothing whatever to do with the works trains, but it may explain why the haze in filling-in details is apparent!

The Works trains are now no more; only the mournful blast of the hooters remains; first one at 06.45 in the morning, then a longish one at 07.20, a short one at 07.25, and a real lengthy blast at 07.30. The hooter itself (or should it be "hooters themselves", for they are two!), are ex-GWR ships' sirens; probably some record exists which names the vessels from which they came. No trains now run into Swindon from three directions at once at 07.20, nor depart in three directions at once at 17.45 in the evening. The workers themselves have probably forgotten them, except when the bus is overcrowded (frequently), or runs late (as frequently) or even not at all. But the men who worked them have not forgotten them.

Paddington to Plymouth 20 years ago

W. J. ALCOCK

JUST OVER twenty years ago, the railways were suffering from the aftermath of an exhausting war. As a result, this was a period of weariness in the speed realm, with journey times considerably longer than in the sprightly 1930s. For example, the best Euston to Glasgow trains took 8 hr 50 min compared to $6\frac{1}{2}$ hr before the war, while the pre-war 4 hr run of the "Cornish Riviera Express" to Plymouth was inflated to a full 5 hr. Nor, under the economic conditions then obtaining was there any immediate prospect of recovery, and as a result the recorder of locomotive performance could not hope to witness anything approaching the lustre of the preceding era, at least, not in the normal course of events. Indeed, he could consider himself lucky if he even managed to arrive on time on the extended schedules then in force. Yet, although this might have seemed a depressing

RIGHT: Grange 4-6-0 No 6802 *Bampton Grange* pilots King Class 4-6-0 No 6021 *King Richard II* with the 06.25 Penzance—Paddington train near Cornwood on August 7, 1956. [T. E. Williams

period to anyone who could remember pre-war glory, there were occasions when flashes of the old brilliance reappeared, if only for a fleeting moment. Such occasions were the 1946 LNER high-speed trial between Kings Cross and Edinburgh, various incidents in the 1948 locomotive exchanges, and isolated feats of time recovery in normal service. Against the background of post-war somnolence, almost anything out of the ordinary could be stimulating, and in retrospect it can be safely said that there was more rejoicing over one good run in those days of speed famine, than in a hundred faster runs in these days of diesel and electric-powered plenty.

In those years, I was living in the city of Plymouth, and as a result, saw a great deal of the Great Western, more especially the main-line to Paddington. No doubt a South Western protagonist would challenge O. S. Nock's statement that the Great Western was "the greatest single institution in the West of England" but the remark certainly has a considerable measure of truth in South Devon and Cornwall. The very mention of railways in this part of Britain evokes memories of strenuous exhausts resounding from the quarries at Stoneycombe, or the tones of a Great Western whistle echoing across the city of Plymouth at night. With mental visions of the lines of chocolate and cream coaches that rolled across Saltash Bridge, or that threaded the lush green Devon countryside, it can be said with little fear of contradiction, that South Devon would not have been the same, without the Great Western.

As an example of the general standard of running over the Plymouth to Paddington main-line at this period I would like to take an occasion in December 1947 an otherwise rather gloomy and depressing period in Great Western history. For one thing, the winds of political change were blowing hard, and nationalisation was less than a month away. For another, it was not long since one of the worst winters in living memory, during which for a time even the "Cornish Rivera" itself had been cancelled. Taken as a whole therefore, the atmosphere was troubled and unsettled conditions of this nature have a habit of affecting all departments and grades of a big organization like a railway. Thus, as I made my way down from Crownhill to Plymouth station (then called North Road) to catch the up "Cornish Riviera Express", I was not at all sure what sort of run I ought to be anticipating. It was a Saturday of wind and rain, when the leaves had nearly all fallen, and winter was fast setting in, an appropriate prelude to a run under somewhat sombre conditions. Yet, after I had bought my ticket, and walked over to No 7 platform, I found the Plymouth portion of the train headed by No 6007 *King William IV*, piloted by Bulldog No 3446 *Goldfinch*. Both engines were surprisingly clean and smart in their Brunswick green, while even on this dull day the light glinted on their gleaming copper and brass work. Moreover, Driver Green and Fireman Page of Old Oak Common who were in charge on the King, were far from depressed, and promised a punctual arrival at Paddington if at all possible. At that time, departure from Plymouth was at 12.15 pm, with an arrival at Paddington $4\frac{3}{4}$ hr later, at 5 pm. This included two stops, one at Exeter, and a previous one at Newton Abbot to detach the pilot, which was provided to give assistance over the heavy South Devon banks. These latter consisted first of the formidable Hemerdon incline, two miles of 1 in 42 from Plympton up to Hemerdon Siding, which came a bare five miles from the start. Any real chance to acquire some speed before the foot of the bank moreover, was frustrated by a service slack to 35 mph round the bend over the bridge across the Plym at Tavistock Junction. The second major obstacle came some 20 miles further on, after traversing the slopes of Dartmoor and descending to the Dart at Totnes. This consisted of the ascent to Dainton, easy enough in its first stages, but steepening in its last mile to an extremely twisty 1 in 38. With gradients of this description, it was little wonder that piloting in South Devon was the rule, rather than the exception, in steam days.

After the Cornish portion of the train had arrived, and its engine, a Castle 4–6–0, had

ABOVE: Manor Class 4-6-0 No 7814 pilots a King Class 4-6-0 on an eastbound express climbing Hemerdon Bank in the summer of 1953. [R. Russell

BELOW: King Class 4-6-0 No 6025 *King Henry III* heads a Plymouth/Paignton—Paddington express along the sea wall at Teignmouth in August 1956. [T. Lewis

run forward, our two locomotives backed the Plymouth portion on, bringing the total load up to 394 tons tare, and 415 tons gross. Such a load was by no means excessive, but in the general conditions prevailing in 1947, it could be sufficient. As an illustration of my point, I could quote an unhappy experience in September 1945 on the down "Cornish Riviera Express" (or "Limited" as it was called colloquially); on that occasion, after a deceptively steady start down to Reading the pace began to slacken markedly up the Kennet Valley, while a pungent reek from an unpleasant trail of smoke gave a strong hint that all was not well on the footplate. By Taunton, no less than three hours had elapsed, and then, for the only time in my experience, we had to stop at Wellington to take rear end assistance up to Whiteball. Our eventual arrival at Plymouth was well over one hour late, the 225.7 miles having occupied some 6 hr. After a demonstration of this nature, which illustrated very amply the baneful effects of bad coal, it seemed to be a temptation of Providence to hope for any larger load than 415 tons to test the capacity of our engine. However, it is important to avoid giving the impression that the Kings could not cope with the adverse conditions of these years, and to restore the balance, it is worth mentioning a magnificent effort I timed on the up "Limited" in December 1948.

The load on this occasion was 359 tons tare, only one ton under the maximum permitted to the Kings when tackling Hemerdon alone. With a fairly full passenger complement the gross load was not less than 380 tons, and this was easily the heaviest load which I saw lifted up the famous incline single handed. Earlier in the same year, during the locomotive exchange trials, LNER Pacific No 60033 *Seagull* had taken 350 tons unassisted, and had made a first class climb, maintaining 18½ mph on the 1 in 42, after recovering from a 25 mph permanent way slack at the bottom. Any speed above 15 mph was impressive towards the top of Hemerdon, without the additional hindrance of a slack at its foot, and there is no doubt that the A4's effort was quite exceptional. Thus, on this run of 1948, I was watching intently to see, now that the opportunity had been vouchsafed, whether the Great Western would be able to equalise the honours. The similarity between the two runs was further increased by the fact that the King, even if it did not have to slow down to 25 through Plympton, had an almost equally hampering slack, because of temporary intensification of the 35 mph restriction over the Plym bridge to 15 mph. Despite this hindrance (and, it should be added, the unwelcome attentions of adverse signals approaching Laira), *King Edward VII* succeeded in reaccelerating the 380 ton "Limited" to 42 mph on the rising gradients to Plympton, and surged through on to the fearsome bank. Up this there were no half measures, and as engine and driver battled with the grade in a driving West Country drizzle, every incremental loss of speed was contested. As we entered the woods half way up, where fallen leaves could wreak havoc with the friction between wheel and rail, speed was still a magnificent 26 mph and the beat from the front was crisp and clear. Then, to add to the drama, Driver Gibbon opened right out, and there was a sudden and violent increase in the noise from the King's exhaust, the thunderous roar of which must have been clearly audible in Crownhill, a good five miles away. To this deafening accompaniment, we scaled the remainder of the bank at nothing less than 18½ mph, a simply splendid achievement which was at least as meritorious as the climb of *Seagull*. By this mighty effort, the "Limited" was heaved up past the signal box at Hemerdon Siding in 15 min 31 sec from Plymouth, and with the worst obstacle over, there were few fears about any of the others. We rolled merrily over Wrangaton summit, descended to the Dart at Totnes, and set out on the rise to Dainton with a pleasant purr from the chimney. On the easier initial stages speed hovered between 45 and 50 mph, and at the exact foot of the 1 in 38 Gibbon opened out suddenly, as before. Then, with the same shattering staccato that we had had on Hemerdon, we carried the pinnacle at almost 30 mph. This description is probably enough to vindicate the reputation of the Kings in the years of adversity, and it is now time to return to that Saturday in December 1947, with *King William IV* and *Goldfinch* blowing off noisily at the eastern end of No 7 Platform, North Road.

At 12.15 pm the whistles sounded, and a sudden silence descended as the regulators were opened and the restive pent-up energy in the boilers was diverted to the cylinders. A moment later, there came a cannon-like blast from the King followed a split second later by a bark from the Bulldog. Soon these explosive acoustics were interweaving with each other in cascade as we pulled up the deep rock cutting to Mutley Tunnel. The sharp blast from the front suddenly became a muffled roar as we entered the short bore, and began the descent through the proletarian Eastern environs of Plymouth. Accelerating rapidly on the down grade, we ran behind the Laira sheds, with their rows of simmering Castles, Halls and Granges, and came out on to the waterside of the muddy Plym estuary. After easing round the bend over the Plym before Tavistock Junction, both drivers opened out to attack the Hemerdon incline. At this stage I was at the window, drinking in the magnificent acoustics, and simultaneously glancing at the swaying tenders ahead, and the oscillating big end of the great connecting rod of the King. There is no doubt that Great Western engines were exceedingly stately machines, and whatever views may or may not have been held at the time on their capacity to deal with post-war coal, they had a first class appearance. Strange to say, appearances often count for more than is commonly realised.

Up the bank we forged with the train slowing perceptibly. Ere we had entered the leafless woods speed had settled down to a steady 16½ mph a conventional pace at this point which, since it was occupying the efforts of two locomotives, serves to emphasize the quality of the run by *King Edward VII*. However, with plenty of power in reserve there were no fears of stalling, and doubtless Green was allowing his engine to warm to its work. Gibbon, on the footplate of *King Edward VII* was on his mettle, since, although he was 1 ton inside the permissible load, he would probably have been regarded as

Manor Class 4-6-0 No 7813 and King Class 4-6-0 No 6003 *King George IV* drift down the straight at the foot of Dainton Bank towards Aller Junction on August 4, 1956. [R. J. Blenkinsop

cutting things a bit fine if he had stalled. As a result, he was probably making absolutely certain, and consequently, his steed was made to develop an effort which exceeded the combined effort of two engines on a more normal run. With the situation well in hand, however, Green surmounted the summit at milepost 239½, and with the exhaust of his, and the pilot engine rapidly quickening, rumbled past Hemerdon signal box in 14 min 14 sec from the start. The countryside out of the carriage window looked desolate and wet as we began to wind steadily up past Cornwood and Ivybridge to Wrangaton, and I settled more comfortably into my warm seat.

Once on the down grades past Wrangaton, speed rose into the low fifties, and it was at 52 that we swung round the sharp curve at Brent, threaded Marley Tunnel, and dipped down Rattery bank to Totnes. On this sharply curved descent there was much braking to restrain the speed, and not until Totnes station hove into view did the grinding noise from underneath the carriages die away. As we rolled through the centre road in exactly 36 min from Plymouth, I heard the exhausts from the engines once more as they set out to tackle the eastbound rise to Dainton. Up the initial easier stretches, speed was sustained at 40–45 mph, but as we hit the final crooked mile at 1 in 38 there came again that rapid deceleration, and that same insistent acoustic beat from the front. At 24 mph we ran up alongside the little siding and into the short Dainton Tunnel, and a moment later were descending past Stoneycombe with the smell of scorching brake blocks. A few minutes later we drew to a stand outside Newton Abbot, in 50 min 52 sec from Plymouth, to drop the pilot.

With the Bulldog detached, *King William IV* recommenced singleheaded, to make the 193.9 mile run to Paddington. To the accompaniment of a beautifully crisp beat, we accelerated to 54 on the level past Kingsteignton, and entered the curving stretch beyond Teignmouth, where the line runs along the sea wall. Here the waves were heaving, green and grey, and ever and anon a shower of spray went up outside the carriage windows. Through the short tunnels we ran, past a rainswept and deserted Dawlish, until we turned away from the sea up the side of the Exe estuary. Far across the stormy flats to our right I could perceive an M7 tank struggling with a long Exmouth branch train, while on the left stretched out the grassy enclosures of Powderham Park. So, at a perfectly steady 60–62 mph we ran through Exminster, and entered the environs of Exeter. Through St Thomas we were braking hard, and at 1.37 pm, 28 min 8 sec after leaving Newton Abbot, we pulled slowly into St Davids.

Here I was treated to the splendid spectacle of Fireman Page making a marathon along the platform to get the footplate tea-can replenished at the buffet—it must have been thirsty work across South Devon! For some reason we were held over time, and it was not until 1.43 pm, 5 min after the published departure that we were away on the 173.6 miles non-stop run to Paddington. Making, once more, a beautifully clean start, Green accelerated his charge through Cowley Bridge Junction, and began the 19 mile ascent to the ridge of the Blackdown Hills at Whiteball. Despite the rain squalls that continually lashed the carriage windows, we were soon making good, if not otherwise spectacular progress. Up the climb at 1 in 155 to Tiverton Junction, speed was held at 50 mph, and in the dip beyond, before Sampford Peverell, it rose to 55 again. The final inclination at 1 in 115 past Burlescombe to the summit did not bring us below 40, and the little signal cabin at the western entrance to Whiteball Tunnel was passed in exactly 26 min for the 19.9 miles.

Down Wellington bank speed rose swiftly to 73 mph and it was good going for 1947 to continue at this rate to Norton Fitzwarren. As we approached Taunton, Green sounded a long fanfare on his whistle, and a few moments later the "Limited" roared through the station at 65 mph. Our time for the 30.8 miles from Exeter was an excellent 36 min 12 sec, and already we were on time.

Eastwards from Taunton, the direct line to

London via Westbury crosses the marshes of Sedgmoor, and then rises by stages to higher ground, until it tops the Mendip ridge at Brewham, east of Bruton. Over the windswept marshes in the driving rain we maintained a steady 66 mph and the rise at 1 in 264 from Curry Rivel Junction up to Somerton Tunnel was carried at 54. On the succeeding undulating stretch to Castle Cary, there was a maximum of 67, and we ran up through Bruton at 55 to attack the broken 1 in 80 to Brewham Summit. On this stiffish gradient, where indifferent steaming could sometimes pull speed down into the twenties, *King William IV* sustained around 40 mph and went over the crest in fine style at an absolute minimum of 37. Before us now was the dip down to the lower ground around the Vale of Pewsey, in which lie the small towns of Frome and Westbury, each by-passed by the railway with a cut-off line.

The short winter's day was now drawing in, and the scene outside was darkening rapidly. Hereabouts the countryside is very open, while to the south there rises the ridge of Salisbury Plain. As we sped on, in the gathering gloom, the sensation of speed increased, as did also the impression of being in the middle of nowhere. In more recent times, the line between Newbury and Taunton has been described as "an economic wilderness" and this was certainly my impression on that run. On easier grades, the rate of travel became lively down past Witham Friary, and remained in the sixties over the two cut-off lines. At Heywood Road Junction, which marks the east end of the Westbury cut-off, we had covered the 78.9 miles from Exeter in 87 min, 23 sec. The 24.5 mile rise to Savernake, the last summit before Paddington now lay immediately ahead.

We started the climb in earnest beyond Edington at 64 mph, and up the ensuing six miles of curved 1 in 222 the minimum was 48, at which speed we topped the rise, at Patney station. From here to Savernake the continuation of the climb is more broken, and there was a recovery to 58 at Pewsey before a final minimum of 51 at Savernake. Up to this point the 103.4 miles had been run in 114 min 14 sec, and we had 83 min left for the final 70.2 miles. This was not a difficult proposition, as long as we had a clear road. Nevertheless, I held my breath metaphorically, for in the realm of punctual arrivals there was many a slip 'tween the cup and the lip in this era.

I need not have feared, however. Through the darkness we ran swiftly down the Kennet Valley, touching 71 as we descended the 1 in 198 from Enborne Junction to Newbury, the latter station appearing as a sudden flurry of light in the outer darkness. Fifteen minutes later we were rounding the bend from Reading West on to the Bristol main line, and greeted by a galaxy of lights which adumbrated journey's end and the approach of the metropolis. We accelerated after the slack from Reading West up the centre road through the General Station, passing the clock in 149 min 26 sec from Exeter, 137.5 miles away. Up that grand road of Isambard Kingdom Brunel we made our stately way, at 60–62 mph until we passed Southall, well poised to make an arrival a good 10 min early. Green, however, evidently thought that this might have been overdoing things, for he eased up as we rolled through Ealing Broadway. From across the wide expanse of tracks, the eyes of suburbia, esconced in a red underground train, saw our proud headboards inscribed "Cornish Riviera Express" decking the smart chocolate and cream carriages as they ran steadily past. The big steel girder overbridges spanning the tracks now came into view against the glow in the sky, and at 4.53 pm, 7 min early, in a running time of 190 min 14 sec from Exeter, we drew to a stand in Paddington.

During the few minutes conversation I had with Green and Page, standing by the massive bulk of *King William IV* I felt that the essence of the run was summed up in their joint contention. "We could have knocked another twenty minutes off if we had wanted to". This, surely, was the spirit of the Great Western, even at the Eleventh Hour. Today? Well the Western diesels run faster and Plymouth is only 210 min from Paddington but I prefer to retain that memory of 1947.

43121

ABOVE: West Country Pacific No 34021 *Dartmoor* takes the curve at Pirbright Junction, between Brookwood and Farnborough, with a down "Cunarder" boat train on July 6, 1967. [Paul Riley

LEFT: Ivatt Class 4 2-6-0 No 43121 leaves a smoke screen across Cumberland as it climbs from Carlisle to Bampton with a special on March 26, 1967. [Paul Riley

Memories of steam

ABOVE: Ivatt Class 4 2-6-0 No 43121 works a featherweight freight on the Langholm branch on July 18, 1967.
[K. Hale

RIGHT: NER Class J27 0-6-0 No 65833 climbs Seaton Bank with coal empties on January 22, 1967.
[Paul Riley

MEMORIES OF STEAM

continued

65833

ABOVE: Privately-preserved WR Castle Class 4-6-0 No 7029 *Clun Castle* works the Stephenson Locomotive Society special marking the end of through services from Paddington to Birkenhead on March 5, 1967. The engine is seen climbing out of Shrewsbury towards Chester. [K. Hale

RIGHT: The southbound "Pines Express", double-headed by LMS Class 2 4-4-0 No 40509 and BR 2-10-0 No 92001, crosses Monkton Combe Viaduct in June, 1961. [G. F. Heiron

MEMORIES OF STEAM

continued

ABOVE: Grange class 4-6-0 No 6813 double-heads Castle class 4-6-0 No 4088 as it leaves Newton Abbot with the 11.05 Paddington—Penzance on September 14, 1957. [T. E. Williams

LEFT UPPER: 43XX 2-6-0 No 5330 leaves Newton Abbot with a Plymouth—Paddington parcels in June, 1958. [D. S. Fish

MEMORIES OF STEAM
concluded

LEFT: Hall Class 4-6-0 No 4936 with the 11.40 Newton Abbot—Kingswear just beats Britannia Pacific No 70019, with the 05.30 Paddington—Penzance, to Aller Junction on November 12, 1955. [Peter W. Gray

RIGHT: 47XX 2-8-0 No 4704 waits to leave Newton Abbot with the 10.20 Paignton—Plymouth after reversal here on July 14 1961. [J. R. Besley

Dirt and leaks in locomotives

W. A. TUPLIN

AFTER ONE has seen how dirty diesels may get, one has less reluctance to reflect on the influence of dirt on the operation of the steam locomotive. It burned coal to boil water, its mechanism needed oil and the rails sometimes needed sand. But the coal it got was never completely combustible, even rain water is not always pure and oil was applied to engines in some places where it was bound to pick up grit. The running of steam locomotives was a perpetual war against dirt and in the end the dirt won.

A big British steam locomotive used a lot of water (very roughly a ton every ten miles) but the water it got contained materials that would not boil away. It was left in the boiler to form sludge that produced hard scale on the heating surface. In a week's normal running, the sludge built up sufficiently to reduce the boiler-power quite markedly. It did this by resisting the passage of heat from the heating surfaces to the water. It therefore caused the metal to get hotter than it would otherwise have been and if this went too far the steel would be softened and dangerously weakened.

So every steam locomotive had to have one day off every week for washing out the boiler. It had to be allowed several hours to cool down; then the boiler was emptied by removing drain plugs at the bottom of the fire-box. Washout-plugs were removed from other parts of the boiler and through the holes long scraper rods were inserted by men who did their best to persuade invisible sludge and scale to come down to exits through which

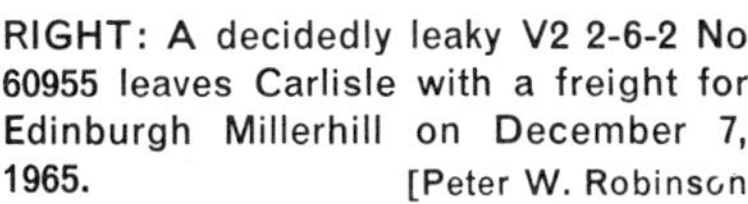

RIGHT: A decidedly leaky V2 2-6-2 No 60955 leaves Carlisle with a freight for Edinburgh Millerhill on December 7, 1965. [Peter W. Robinson

LEFT: An equally-troubled WD 2-8-0 No 90112; maintaining joints and glands steam tight could make all the difference between a locomotive in good order and one which could barely work a train. [L. A. Nixon

they were washed out by flowing water. It was not a hundred per cent process, and when a locomotive boiler was finally scrapped, a hundredweight of stratified stones up to 2 in square and ½ in thick might be found in the bottom of the water-spaces.

After washing out, and after screwing in all the washout plugs, the boiler was refilled with water, a fire was started on the grate and the re-attainment of working pressure could take eight hours because it was always held that quick warming-up would damage the boiler.

The amount of solid matter left in the boiler by boiling water depended very much on where the water came from and on the chemicals (if any) that had been added to it before it reached the boiler. In principle it was possible to identify the solids dissolved in the water, to ascertain their concentration and to add such chemicals as to precipitate the non-water so that it could be mechanically separated from the water. In practice this was attempted but could not be done precisely. In the later years of the steam locomotive this subject was pursued more intensely by Louis Armand on French Railways than it had been done before and the TIA treatment could enable the interval between consecutive washouts to be multiplied by five or more.

Solid matter left in boilers by water was in general chemically alkaline, but some water was acidic and could corrode steel rather rapidly. In some circumstances, waters of opposite chemical characteristics could be set against each other by appropriately transferring from one district to another locomotives that did not run very far from base. An engine with a new boiler might first work in an alkaline water district so that its heating surfaces became coated with scale and with the metal thus protected the engine could then be transferred to an acid water district. By systematic circulation of locomotives between different sheds, none of them suffered the worst conditions continuously.

Although the dirt in boiler feed-water could be dangerous there was much less of it than there was of dirt associated with the coal. The immediately obvious dirt was coal dust and the immediate sufferer was the fireman, especially when the job was so hard as to leave him little time for spraying water onto the coal on the tender. There was usually plenty of draught in the cab when the engine was running and both men were apt to get well blackened when there was no time to spray dusty coal. Only a small proportion of British tenders had pipes permanently fixed for spraying the coal.

In the sudden heat of the fire the surface of the coal was apt to divide in fine flakes that were drawn through the tubes towards the chimney and might not be burned up on the way. If not, they might be shot out of the chimney or might drop to the bottom of the smokebox and remain there in a half-burnt condition.

Eventually every piece of coal in the firebox burned down to a size so small that the draught might lift it off the fire and through the tubes, to be caught by the smokebox or to leave it by way of the chimney.

The smokebox thus gradually amassed a great deal of half-burned coal (char) in pieces of nearly uniform size and eventually these had to be removed because otherwise they would block an intolerably large proportion of the tubes. The char collected in the smokebox could amount to 10 per cent of the coal fed into the firebox. Another 10 per cent might be thrown out of the chimney.

At the end of each day (or more frequently) the char (mixed with coal dust and coke dust) was shovelled out of the smokebox into a heap alongside the reception line at an engine shed. Eventually it would be shovelled up into a wagon to be taken away for disposal elsewhere. Each shovelling operation meant much spreading of dust by wind.

The first shovelling could be eliminated (on many locomotives) by providing a chute leading from the bottom of the smokebox to the track. Certain classes of locomotive were thus provided, but the chute was usable only when the engine was standing where there was a pit of suitable depth between the rails. The system was never extensively used because removal of the char from a pit was even more difficult than removing it from the track side.

At some British engine sheds there was a section of track over a wet ashpit from which ash dropped from ash-pans was removed by mechanical means. In such a place the char from a smokebox chute could be handled efficiently, but elsewhere the chute could not justify itself.

Emptying an ash pan was one of the most unpleasant jobs at an engine shed. Someone had to go into a pit between the rails under an engine and to use a long-handled scraper to draw towards himself hot ash, dust and clinker (fused ash) so that it fell into the pit a yard or so away from his feet. Only a small proportion of British steam locomotives had hopper-type ashpans that could be emptied without requiring anyone to go under the engine.

Extraction and disposal of dirt was a major operation at engine sheds and in Britain it was never mechanised to the extent that was physically possible, simply because in the days before the second world war there was no special difficulty in finding manual labour for it. After the second world war this ceased to be the case and this was one of the circumstances that contributed to the abandonment of steam.

A device that came here from America in the war-time 2-8-0s was the self-cleaning smokebox. This contained plates shaped and situated so that the gas-flow inside the smokebox guided most of the char out of the chimney. This relieved shed-staff of one job (or most of it) but lineside householders suffered in consequence. Self-cleaning smokeboxes did not harm many people on the American prairies but they were a bit unkind in suburbia.

Dirt may be defined as matter in a place where it is a nuisance. Leakage may be defined as the escape of liquid or gas from a place where it can be useful to a place where it cannot. In a locomotive there could be leakages of water, oil, air or steam. Some leakages caught the eye easily; others could not be detected by any eye, however penetrating.

Immediately obvious leakage of steam was from glands on piston rods or from joint faces on the cylinder block. Not only could a steam cloud be easily seen, but it might be big enough to restrict the driver's view of where he was going. This was detestable and dangerous besides being wasteful and such faults were usually corrected quickly.

But steam that leaked past pistons and valves got away in the exhaust steam and no eye could see it. If it became great enough such leakage might be detected, or at least suspected, by examination of the coal-consumption figures. If excessive consumption vanished on renewal of piston-rings and valve-rings, it was reasonable to suppose that a substantial fraction of the steam supplied to the valve-chests had been getting away past worn piston-rings and valve-rings without doing any useful work.

Invisible leakage of steam could be severe enough to invalidate conclusions deduced from the results of comparative tests. For example, in a compound engine, leakage of steam past the high pressure pistons and valves was not very important because the steam was caught by the low-pressure cylinders. It was leakage past the low pressure pistons and valves that mattered and such leakage tended to be small because the pressure was low. So if it were found that a compound engine burned rather less coal than did a simple engine, the difference may well have been due to the smaller leakage rather than to the compound principle. What were intended to be comparisons between locomotives might be in fact only comparisons between their leaks.

Air that leaked into a smokebox could spoil the draught to the extent that the engine would not steam, that is to say it was impossible to maintain the full working pressure in the boiler while the engine was keeping time or was doing its best towards keeping time.

The application of superheating to steam locomotives was shown to be able to reduce coal-consumption by about 25 per cent. But it placed in the smokebox about 60 joints through which high pressure steam might leak. A small leakage at any one of those joints might make little difference to the coal consumption but by spoiling the draught in the smokebox it could reduce the power of the locomotive by anything up to 20 per cent.

Water leakages in locomotives or tenders were not usually great enough to be more than inconveniences. Boiler-water might escape past stay-heads into the firebox in fine jets that might be seen when the engine was standing with a very low fire, but not when the fire was lively. (Some men thought that the heat closed up the leak!) Such jets might be a nuisance to a man who had to work inside the firebox while there was steam pressure in the boiler. In some cases he might find it necessary to have an umbrella, but this was not common.

Steam locomotives were normally lubricated on the total loss principle and the only disadvantage of oil leakage was that it might empty an oil reservoir during the course of a long non-stop run. If a bearing ran hot in consequence, the non-stop run might not be as long as the time-table possibly suggested.

As sand, like oil, was also used on the total loss principle, the main disadvantage of leakage was depletion of the stock, but sand could be detrimental if it leaked onto sliding surfaces. This was unlikely with sand-boxes down at axle-box level and the commonest trouble with sand was not that it flowed through unintended openings but that it sometimes refused to flow where a clear passage had been left for it.

Dirt and leaks were perpetual nuisances to steam locomotives, but it was exceedingly rare for either of them to put an engine suddenly and completely out of action. What are the gremlins that continually shoot down the diesels?

BELOW: One of the delights of steam locomotive working was keeping it clean, particularly when components were covered in oily muck as on this BR Class 5 4-6-0. [M. Dunnett

Metroland in 1916

T. B. PEACOCK

IT IS SUMMER: some say they can hear gunfire in France. From Uxbridge, still a quiet market town, a war-time train service will take us to Baker Street, a distance of just under 17 miles. Though becoming less frequent, the service is still good, and fundamentally similar to that of two years ago. The station for departure belongs to the Metropolitan Railway Company. The approach is by means of a separate carriageway leading from Belmont Road; but unlike the two Great Western stations, the Metropolitan terminus has never been distinguished, officially, by the name of the road. Incorporating the stationmaster's house, the building is pleasingly designed, and is substantially constructed of local yellow brick relieved with red facings. The

BELOW: The former Metropolitan terminus at Uxbridge, originally used by the Metropolitan and District Railways. After the formation of London Transport, Piccadilly Line trains replaced the District services, as seen here on October 23, 1933. Later a new station was built at Uxbridge for LT trains.
[London Transport

conventional-style roof is clad with plain red tiles. Ornamental roof timbers add decorative warmth to a lofty, spacious booking-hall. Of the two platforms, the southern, amply wide and well protected, is reserved for Metropolitan trains. The other, unfurnished except for a green-painted wooden shelter, is for the sole use of the District Railway Company, which operates a basic service of one-car 'trains' to and from South Acton. We take our places in one of the brown, wood-panelled saloon coaches of the Metropolitan train due to leave at 9.45 am. Every now and then, the brake motor sets up a vibrant throb, and then, with a sigh, lapses into silence. The stealthy arrival of the District company's little red car at the north platform denotes that within a minute we should be off.

A strident trill from the guard's whistle, his green flag waving, and we glide out of the station to the light drone of the motors, and immediately cross to the up line. A steam locomotive is shunting in the huge expanse of goods and marshalling yards to the right. We pass into a deep, wide cutting spanned by a high bridge with four arches, elegantly proportioned, which carries Park Road across the railway. The bridge is built of local yellow brick interspersed with courses of blue, which embellish the curve of each arch. Of the two centre arches, that to the north accommodates the running lines and the southern one embraces two tracks that form the shunting neck for the goods yard. Helped by a sharply falling gradient, we quickly gather speed, rocked gently from side to side. Leaving the cutting, we have a fine view from a curved embankment of rolling hills and rich brown ploughland and corn-fields, while on the right is parkland studded with oaks of great age, some sheltering white-painted bee-hives. Ours is a branch-line stopping train, and its swift, comfortable progress is all too soon interrupted by the siss-siss of the brake mechanism as the carriages are brought to a standstill at the first stopping-place.

Ickenham, of timber construction, with a small improvised booking-office, is still classified as a halt. An irksome characteristic of its surroundings is the constant, high-pitched buzzing from an electricity sub-station adjacent to the line. A screen of poplars intensifies the shade cast by surrounding trees. Within a minute of leaving Ickenham, we pass beneath the four-rail span of the Great Western & Great Central Joint railway, with its array of Great Western signals at the eastern approach to Ruislip & Ickenham Station.

On, through a shallow cutting, we come to Ruislip Station. It is of red brick with stone facings, and the main offices are on the north platform. Verandahs to both are supported by ornamental ironwork. East of the down platform, a full-scale signalbox controls the only intermediate block-post in normal use on the branch. Carried upon a rising embankment to a level above them, the line flanks a goods yard and sidings on our left for virtually the whole distance between Ruislip and Ruislip Manor. Here a halt serves a housing estate in course of development on the Garden City principle, a concept coming into favour.

The cutting through which the line continues to the next stopping-place is just deep enough to conceal a view of the surrounding countryside. Timber-built, similar to Ickenham, Eastcote Halt is half-a-mile south of the village it serves. The booking office is a small wooden hut beside a narrow, stone-surfaced road, from where a cinder path leads down the embankment to the up platform in the cutting. Access to that on the down side is over the road bridge and down a similar track. Abutting the roadside further on is a siding, used chiefly for agricultural produce. Its junction with the running line is two or three hundred yards east of the halt and protected by lower quadrant signals operated from a miniature cabin. Except on the rare occasions when the siding is visited by a steam locomotive, the block-post is switched out.

Between Eastcote Halt and Rayner's Lane, there are no houses within sight of the railway. Flanking the line is the typical, flat Middlesex countryside with overgrown hedges enclosing irregular-shaped fields of tumble-down pasture, some coming under the plough as a wartime measure. Rayner's Lane is the smallest halt on the branch, otherwise similar to Ickenham and Eastcote. Ruislip Manor and West Harrow, both more recent, have a somewhat ampler, more modern mode of construction. At the road bridge over the line east of Rayner's Lane Halt, the branch which diverges southward carries District trains on to their own railway by an end-on junction with the Metropolitan at South Harrow.

Our train moves slowly over an up gradient, calling at West Harrow, before joining the Metropolitan main line at Harrow North Junction. A goods depot and marshalling yard, complete with every facility, together extend almost the whole distance between the stations at North Harrow and Harrow-on-the-Hill, and shunting over them hour after hour is a Great Western saddle-tank engine in brown Metropolitan livery. South of the line, parts of the embankment have been planted as war-time allotments. A falling gradient brings us quickly into Platform 2 at Harrow-on-the-Hill.

"All change, all change—Number Four, Baker Street" is the cry; and urgent feet patter up the stairs, over the wooden foot-bridge and down to No 4, the most northerly platform. Oddly, the bay at the extreme south of the station is excluded from the platform numbering, a shortcoming confusing to passengers not versed in railway nomenclature. From platform 2, the branch train shunts to No 1 line to enter the bay for the return journey. Meanwhile a crowd is massed on No 4 platform, everyone jostling for a position from which to storm the incoming train for London. It arrives almost on time, a heterogeneous rake hauled by one of the Company's tank engines. She comes clanking in as though played out with exertion, steam weeping from the safety-valve and whistle, relieved by the down gradient on which to put up a show of speed into the station. As the carriages are eagerly seized by the waiting throng, the engine retires to the coaling stage, to be replaced by an electric locomotive, coming in from an adjoining spur, silent, efficient, modern.

The horn is sounded. We quickly gather speed and move rapidly down the Hill. A deep, wide cutting melts away to reveal a wide expanse of open country as we cross the six-line span of the London & North Western Railway, with Kenton Station discernible to the north. In some of the fields we pass are huge wooden hoardings: "Carter's Little Liver Pills," "Beecham's Pills Worth a Guinea a Box," and the effigies of two white-coated decorators cheerfully carrying brushes, pails and plank to begin their next job with Hall's distemper. Curving southward on an embankment, we flick past a timber halt called Preston Road, to the quick, rhythmic beat of the wheels consonant with the text of miniature advertisements in our saloon coach, "Get it at Harrods, Get it at Harrods." So we go swiftly on, through the hot summer sunshine, into the grimy haze which permeates the vast, ugly fabric of the City's high-pressure suburbs. Alongside us the Great Central Railway bypasses all the stations through which we rush. They go by with such speed and frequency that we can scarcely keep count of them: Wembley Park, Neasden for Kingsbury, Dollis Hill, Willesden Green, Kilburn & Brondesbury, West Hampstead, and Finchley Road, the last daylight station.

The line now burrows into a mountainous hillside with all the paraphernalia of urban life upon it. Two underground stations we pass, Swiss Cottage and Marlborough Road, have the air of a bygone age, so little have they changed in fifty years, their lamps still framed in big, glass globes of Victorian design. Stout, snake-like cables, seeming to writhe along the tunnel walls, tease and fascinate the eye. On leaving St John's Wood Road Station, we glimpse the Great Central again, where giant locomotives snooze in front of the terminus. In the murky daylight approach to Baker Street Station, we are reminded that colour-light signals have not yet wholly replaced the semaphores, described by one writer as "the stumpy, vulgar-looking little signals of the Baker Street company."

At 10.27 we draw into the up through platform at the Metropolitan Railway's

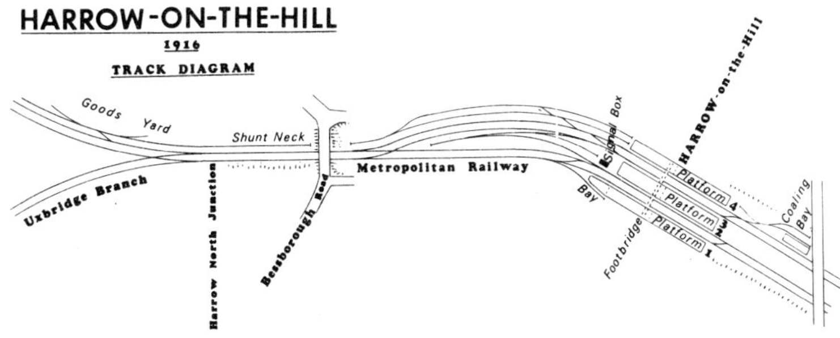

RIGHT: Track plan of Harrow-on-the-Hill Station in 1916.

headquarters. So ends an unromantic journey at one of the dullest of all dull London stations. No architectural merit here, nothing we shall ever wish to preserve for prosterity. Yet this is a station that may always be with us just as it is; good, plain, work-a-day Baker Street.

Metroland: A name coined for publicity purposes, referring to territory served by the Metropolitan Railway.

The station for departure: Originally that of the Harrow & Uxbridge Railway Company, which was absorbed by the Metropolitan on June 30, 1905. Opened July 4, 1904 for regular steam trains. First electric train, December 13, 1904; regular service from January 1, 1905.

"trains" to and from South Acton: The District service began on March 1, 1910, hourly except at peak periods, when multi-coach units were provided—a few to and from the City. District trains to Uxbridge were replaced on October 23, 1933 by those of the Piccadilly Line tube, many working to and from Cockfosters.

marshalling yards: A new terminus, fronting the High Street, was opened on December 4, 1938. Access through the site of the goods yard effected great savings in the acquisition of property and the demolition of buildings.

shunting neck: The running-lines have since been transposed.

first stopping-place: Hillingdon was added on December 10, 1923.

Ruislip Station: At first, the only intermediate stopping-place on the branch. Ickenham was added on September 25, 1905, and Eastcote and Rayner's Lane on May 26, 1906.

Ruislip Manor: Opened as a halt, 640 yd east of Ruislip Station, on August 5, 1912. Closed February 12, 1917 to March 31, 1919 inclusive and on Sundays until May 6, 1928. Present station completed June 26, 1938.

Eastcote: Reconstructed as station in 1939.

tumble-down pasture: Technically, a temporary ley which has been allowed to "tumble down" into coarse "permanent pasture" by self-sowing. Frequently encountered on fields earmarked for building.

Rayner's Lane: The full-size station, of permanent construction, was opened on August 8, 1938.

West Harrow: Opened as timber-built halt on November 17, 1913.

Great Western saddle-tank: One of two former GWR Peckett engines, numbered 101 and 102, in use on the Metropolitan Railway between 1912 and 1920.

Harrow North Junction: Harrow to Pinner opened May 25, 1885.

Harrow-on-the-Hill: Opened on completion of the line from Baker Street on August 2, 1880.

tank engines: E Class (0-4-4T), designed by T. F. Clark, C.M.E., and built between 1896 and 1901.

Preston Road: Opened as a halt on May 20, 1908.

Swiss Cottage: Opened April 13, 1868: closed August 18, 1940.

Marlborough Road: Opened April 13, 1868: closed November 20, 1939.

vulgar-looking little signals: *The Daily News*, December 29, 1898—"Character in Railway Signals".

5428

ABOVE: Princess in action; former LMS Pacific No 6201 *Princess Elizabeth* works one of the special trains run in Tyseley Yard on September 28, 1969 for the Open Day. [J. W. Ellson

Steam alive on the standard gauge

LEFT: For the Tyseley Open Day on May 17, 1970, LMS Class 5 4-6-0 No 5428 was used on the shuttle passenger service in Tyseley Yard. [J. H. Cooper-Smith

BELOW: King Class 4-6-0 No 6000 *King George V* is able to display some of its powers in sidings at Bulmers Yard, Hereford, where it is seen with part of the company's cider train on April 4, 1969. [J. H. Cooper-Smith

ABOVE: Bluebell Railway Class E4 0-6-2T No 473 *Birch Grove* shunts stock at Horsted Keynes on August 9, 1970. [D. A. Idle

TOP LEFT: Memories of Kings Cross are captured by this shot of preserved Gresley Class N2 0-6-2T No 4744 as it storms away from Haworth with the 12.55 Keighley—Oxenhope on March 31, 1970. [Ian G. Holt

LEFT: Another view of the KWVR, this time with Class USA 0-6-0T No 72 with the Sunday 14.50 Haworth —Oxenhope on January 4, 1970. [John M. Boyes

RIGHT: Although passenger services have not been restored under formal arrangements on the Goathland—Grosmont North Yorkshire Moors line, members trains have been run on special occasions. Class Q6 0-8-0 No 3395 heads the 15.10 Ellerbeck—Grosmont on August 31, 1970. [D. A. Idle

ABOVE: Dart Valley 0-4-2T No 1420 leaves Staverton Bridge with the 18.05 Totnes—Buckfastleigh train on July 15, 1970. [John M. Boyes

TOP RIGHT: DVR 0-6-0PT No 6413 coasts alongside the River Dart approaching Staverton on August 13, 1969. [G. P. Cooper

RIGHT: Newly restored Stanier 2-8-0 No 8233 waits at Bridgnorth with a train for Hampton Loade on May 24, 1970. [P. Berry

LEFT: Ivatt Class 4 2-6-0 No 43106 passes Daniels Mill with the 12.00 Bridgnorth—Hampton Loade on May 24, 1970. [A. G. Cattle

The Isle of Man Railway yesterday and today

ABOVE: Douglas Station on June 13, 1968 with 2-4-0T No 12 standing on the engine release road and No 8 adding a coach to the 11.20 train at Port Erin. [G. D. King

TOP LEFT: Isle of Man Railway yesterday, with No 12 *Hutchinson* in its red livery at Port St Mary with the 14.15 from Douglas on June 16, 1965. [L. Freeman

LEFT: For a short while after the re-constitution of the railway in 1968, the Ramsey line was operated; IoMR No 12 heads the 10.20 from Douglas to Ramsey at Devils Elbow on June 21, 1968. [G. D. King

ABOVE: An exceptional working on the Isle of Man, with No 10 *G. H. Wood* arriving at Castletown with an 11 coach train of empty stock. This was to work a special for international visitors to the Isle of Man on April 25, 1962. No 5 assisted at the rear of the train.
[P. H. Groom

LEFT: The 10.20 to Peel and Ramsey leaves Douglas on July 17, 1968 double-headed by two unidentified 2-4-0Ts.
[M. Dunnett

RIGHT: IoMR No 10 is reflected in the River Neb with a train from Peel to Douglas on May 27, 1962.
[P. H. Groom

THE ISLE OF MAN RAILWAY YESTERDAY AND TODAY

continued

LEFT: A panoramic view overlooking Peel, with a train from Douglas arriving in the foreground on July 23, 1968. [M. Dunnett

ABOVE: Another view of No 10, this time in green livery on June 20, 1968 with the 10.20 Douglas—Peel, photographed near Braddon. [G. D. King

THE ISLE OF MAN RAILWAY YESTERDAY AND TODAY

concluded

BELOW: No 10 coasts into Castletown with the 14.05 Douglas—Port Erin, as No 11, with the 14.15 Port Erin—Douglas, waits in the loop on June 24, 1968. [G. D. King

Alfred Jee - an early engineer

N. W. WEBSTER

ALFRED JEE was one of the brilliant young engineers whose work followed that of the original great members of the railway revolution: George and Robert Stephenson, Brunel, Locke and Vignoles. His name is not mentioned by Samuel Smiles, for long recognised as the only authority on engineers and railways, and it is only the more careful scholarship of recent years which has brought his name to the fore. Like Locke, whose pupil he was, his genius was apparent at an early age but it was a bitter turn of fate which robbed him and his brother of their lives at the moment of triumph.

He was born in Liverpool on August 2, 1816, the son of a prosperous merchant, Matthew Jee, given the Christian names of Alfred Stanistreet and sent to school at the Royal Institution in Colquitt Street in the city where his tutor Dr Tattershall soon saw that he had a pupil of especial talent. Like his future master Locke, who also studied part-time at the Institution during his residence in Liverpool, Alfred showed exceptional ability as a mathematician and combined his theoretical knowledge with manual dexterity. As a young lad he constructed working models and machines of some complexity, a gift which he developed and pursued for the rest of his life. Model making became for him an enjoyable hobby of which he never tired.

With such gifts it is not surprising that he decided in his early 'teens to become an engineer. His father had a merchant's residence at Edge Hill, two miles from the city centre, and Alfred was thus able to see the planning construction and opening of the Liverpool & Manchester Railway. The first passenger terminus at the Liverpool end of the railway was at Crown Street yard, but a tunnel branched off at Edge Hill to the docks at Wapping by Merseyside. Once the line proved successful a second bore was driven from Edge Hill to a new terminus in the city centre at Lime Street. Joseph Locke was George Stephenson's assistant on the western end of

LEFT: Warrington viaduct over the River Mersey and the Mersey & Irwell Canal on completion in 1837. Designed by Locke, it was Jee's first major work as resident engineer. It is still in use.

ABOVE: A broadside view of Etherow Viaduct near Mottram on the Sheffield, Ashton-under-Lyne and Manchester Railway planned by Vignoles, designed by Locke and built by Jee. This view was taken from a painting by J. M. Baines made in 1846 and now at Clapham Museum.

the line and it fell to his lot to complete both these tunnels and, incidentally, to rectify some serious errors inherited from his predecessors.

Alfred was thus able to see the development of some of the most interesting engineering features of the world's first public locomotive-powered railway. He sought the acquaintance of Locke, either through the Royal Institution or at the offices of the railway in Liverpool, and in 1831 at the age of 15 was appointed his pupil, to serve the statutory term of seven years. There is ample evidence that Locke saw the boy's qualities from the start; much of his own success was derived from his ability to recognise, train and develop new talent.

On August 12, 1835 Joseph Locke was appointed engineer-in-chief of the Grand Junction, Britain's first trunk line, then under construction between Warrington and Birmingham, thereby supplanting his old master George Stephenson. The two previous years had seen an unhappy partnership between the two with Locke showing a mastery of the engineering work involved, outshining Stephenson who was nominally in charge. A growing bitterness in the relationship had not helped and Stephenson was further enraged when he was demoted to the role of consultant. On September 16, 1835, he resigned completely from the Grand Junction leaving Locke in supreme command. The truth was that both men were leaders; neither could serve in the role of subordinate. Locke was free to pursue his own incisive methods and to appoint his own staff. Thomas Brassey was given his first chance as contractor on the Penkridge viaduct and Jee was made resident engineer for the Warrington viaduct. He was scarcely 19 years old, incredibly young for such a responsible task, but Locke himself had laid out the Black Fell mineral line in County Durham at the same age.

Although the Warrington viaduct was by no means the greatest work on the line, it was a key feature and both Locke and his Company were anxious to see its construction brought to a successful conclusion. The directors of the Grand Junction, the Liverpool Party of financiers, had accepted in the Act (3 & 4 Wm. 4, cap. 34, May 6, 1833) that the viaduct should be "firm and substantial" in construction. In his approach to Warrington from the south Locke had to cross the River Mersey and the Irwell & Mersey canal. He chose a point where the two were closely parallel and decided on a single viaduct of 12 arches at a height of 30 ft above the water level. A single arch of 40 ft crossed the canal while two elliptical arches of 75 ft spanned the river. Great attention was paid to the efficiency and appearance of the design and to the construction; sandstone was prescribed for the building material; the piers of the large arches were carried down to the underlying rock while the smaller ones were secured by piles driven deep into the ground.

Jee therefore had no simple river bridge to construct but a work of some complexity. The area was still rural, in contrast to its present appearance, and the Mersey, a meandering stream ("like a beautiful coquette graceful even in extravagance" says a contemporary guide-book), liable to flood the surrounding meadows in winter, turning the area into a great spreading marsh. He superintended the building with all the competence of his master and teacher, finishing the viaduct on time. The work was certainly pleasing in appearance, as the accompanying illustration shows, the topographer Thomas Roscoe writing enthusiastically of it: "This splendid structure is one of the great attractions of the Grand Junction Railway." It remains as built to this day, neglected like most of our railway monuments, but as sound as ever. Although the old viaduct is still in use, the present main line is taken a little to the west on a slope of 1 in 135 in its approach to the higher crossing of the later Manchester Ship Canal.

Jee's first major work seems to have established him as Locke's favourite pupil, and he participated in many of the growing number of his master's projects. When his pupilage expired in 1838 Locke appointed him resident engineer for the Lancaster & Preston Railway, a fairly straightforward project of about 20 miles in length near the course of the old mail coach route. The present M6 motorway follows the line on the eastern side and it is interesting to see how Jee's original bridges on this section have been extended to cross the line of motorway. Alfred's success in his career influenced his younger brother Morland who joined him as pupil and assistant.

When Jee had completed the Lancaster & Preston in 1840 Locke switched him to the greater difficulties of the Sheffield & Manchester which he had taken over from Vignoles in May 1839. For over five years Alfred's attentions were directed at this line, where he shouldered many of the heavy responsibilities that had fallen on Locke. He at first was involved in the driving of the notorious Woodhead tunnel but also acted as resident engineer for the great Dinting Vale and Etherow viaducts. Locke had redesigned Vignoles's original works and had specified his favourite laminated timber arches set in stone piers, as he did later for his Seine and Lune bridges. Both viaducts were designed and completed with remarkable speed. Jee ended his considerable work in this area by constructing the Huddersfield & Manchester, and Huddersfield & Sheffield Railways. He remained their engineer until his death and the resolution which the Board passed on that occasion and communicated to his widow expressed their high appreciation of his abilities. As a result of his work in Yorkshire he was elected a member of the Institution of Civil Engineers in 1844.

Jee's great chance to establish himself as an engineer of international repute came in 1851. Locke himself had built the first railway in Spain, from Barcelona to Mataro, and although it is not stated Alfred presumably had accompanied him on that occasion (1847). In any event, in the year of the Great Exhibition Jee's advice was sought by the Spanish Government on a project to connect the port of Santander on the north coast with the line of the Castile canal at Coralles. Accepting the commission with enthusiasm Jee moved to

Santander, not only surveying possible routes but producing detailed plans and designs for the engineering features, and for rolling stock as well. The countryside was of the most difficult character, consisting of lines of mountains and deep valleys, and Jee's earlier work in the Pennines proved invaluable.

All Alfred's experience and qualities now came to the fore. He learned Spanish with extraordinary rapidity and was able to converse fluently, using all the necessary technical terms, with his Spanish fellow engineers. There is no doubt that this additional attribute secured their confidence and his appointment as engineer to the undertaking was confirmed, with Morland nominated as his assistant. He had learned well from Locke, whose forte was careful planning and attention to detail. A memoir on Jee's work in Spain in the Institution of Civil Engineers states: "His skill in design, the accuracy and completeness of the details, and his thorough practical experience, were strongly evinced on this railway, where every work was minutely tested by the Spanish Government engineers; and the result was the establishment of a high reputation amongst the Spaniards, not only for his skill as an engineer, but for the strictest probity and honesty of purpose in all his transactions."

The constructional work through such difficult terrain was arduous and protracted and it was not until March 1857 that Alfred and Morland Jee were able to open the first part of their line, 35 miles in the central section from Reinosa to Alas del Rey in the district of Palencia. But the difficulties were being resolved and not much more than a year later the time had come to open the second section. The Spaniards were delighted at their new railway and proud of their engineers; colourful preparations had been made for the inaguration; among other embellishments an arch of evergreen trees bearing the word SUCCESS had been erected across the track. It was as the train approached this arch that disaster struck; both brothers Jee were on the footplate of the engine, which they were driving slowly on a newly formed embankment. A slight incident began the tragedy; the crowd saw with horror that the weight of the train was causing some slipping of the bank. The effect was slight but sufficient to tilt the engine which was derailed, overturned and thrown 25 ft down the slope. Alfred was crushed by the driving wheel of the engine and died instantly; Morland, who was severely burned, died ten days later in hospital but the rest of those injured eventually recovered.

The Jees were deeply mourned in Spain and when Alfred's body was shipped back to Liverpool on September 7, 1858, a solemn ceremony attended by hundreds of mourners marked the sad occasion. "With mute eloquence of grief they bid adieu for ever to the remains of the talented engineer," reported the *Santander Journal* on the next day. "The true friend and the honourable man, who leaves in this foreign land a grateful and imperishable memory of his talents and virtues, and a sad remembrance of his unfortunate end. If to his relatives and those at a distance it is any alleviation to know the interest and deep feeling which has been shown in Santander, we can announce to them that it has been general, and that the melancholy act of the last farewell has been celebrated with all merited respect and with every possible honour."

So died Alfred Jee in his 42nd year at the pinnacle of his career, to be mourned by his wife and children and by his fellow engineers in Spain and Britain. The manner of his death and that of his brother is a reminder of the hazards which the early railway engineers faced, for they were personally involved with their railway projects. It is an interesting, if vain, exercise to wonder what the Jees might have made of their lives if they had been spared. Under normal circumstances they might have had 20 or 30 years of life before them, years in which they would have passed into the more advanced phase of railway technology. The Settle-Carlisle route, the drive to the north of Scotland, new lines perhaps in Canada or India, might have been theirs; but they lie forgotten in a Liverpool cemetery and the lines which they built serve as their only memorial.

The Gysev Railway—an independent international railway

A RADIO FREE EUROPE FEATURE

A TINY international railway, believed the only one of its kind in Europe, recently celebrated its 90th anniversary and received official word that it can look forward to at least another 20 years of existence.

Called the Gysev, the railway is unique in that it is a privately-owned line that operates in both Communist Hungary and neutral Austria without being a part of either country's state railway system.

The Gysev is formally known as the Raab–Oedenburg–Ebenfurther Eisenbahn in Austria and the Gyoer–Sporon–Ebenfurti Vasut in Hungary. The name Gysev comes from the initial letters of the Hungarian designation.

The line has a track length of only 217 km, stretching from Gyoer (Raab in German), a major rail centre about 100 km west of Budapest, to the Austrian town of Ebenfurth, a few kilometres south of Vienna. A branch line runs between Neusiedl and Pamhagen, both of which are in a finger of Austria projecting eastward just north of the Hungarian border town of Sopron.

Its original charter was granted in October 1879, during the heyday of the Austro-Hungarian Empire. The franchise, for "a private railway connecting the Austrian town of Ebenfurth with the Hungarian town of Gyoer," was for 90 years. Both countries recently granted the company an extension of its operating franchise for another 20 years.

In its first 90 years of existence, the Gysev survived two world wars, political intrigues, revolution, military occupation and the Iron Curtain barriers of the cold war era. But perhaps the greatest blow to the hopes of the Gysev's founders came in its early days when Austrian political intrigue prevented it from becoming a part of the main north–south rail line between Vienna and Ljubljana, in present-day Yugoslavia. Ljubljana was then part of the Kingdom of Hungary.

Rather than route the main line through Sopron and other Hungarian lands, Austrian interests in the court of Emperor Franz Joseph managed to have a completely new line built, one that passed through Austria's Semmering Pass and avoided Hungarian territory until it crossed into Croatia.

But the Gysev survived this loss of potential income and moved ahead gradually, despite the fact it had been bypassed as a major international railway route. It steadily increased its passenger and freight traffic and by 1918 it was carrying 2.4 million passengers a year.

In the turbulent days following the first world war, much of the territory served by the Gysev shifted back and forth between Austria and Hungary as international commissions readjusted the frontiers of the now-divided halves of the former empire. After a plebiscite in 1921, Sopron (Oedenburg in German), which was one of the Gysev's main stations, was awarded to Hungary. The new border also cut across the Neusiedl–Pamhagen branch line, which originally was linked to the main track at the Hungarian town of Fertoesszentimiklos.

At the close of the second world war, the Gysev found itself with heavy damage to both its trackage and station buildings, incurred during the retreat of the German army and the advance of Soviet troops. Forced to shut down completely for a time, the line resumed restricted operations, mostly carrying Soviet troops and supplies in 1945. Civilian trains began running again in 1946.

After the disruptions caused by the Soviet occupation of eastern Austria, the Communist takeover in Budapest and the Hungarian revolution of 1956, the Gysev began to prosper again. It rejoined the international rail network and obtained an increasing amount of passenger and freight business. In 1968, for instance, it carried more than 6 m passengers and 5.2 m tons of freight.

Officials say the Gysev's volume of traffic is expected to grow even more as east–west communication increases. The line will play an increased role in the transit handling of Soviet consignments to West Germany and Italy.

The company, which has its headquarters in Budapest, is also modernising its present equipment and planning to expand into other fields. Dieselisation of the Hungarian section is expected to be completed by 1975. The company is building an international bonded warehouse at Sopron to facilitate east–west freight shipments. It also plans to establish its own motor truck transport firm and to build a spa hotel for western tourists at Heviz, in Hungary's Lake Balaton resort area. Moreover, the Gysev is planning to extend its rail service from the present eastern terminal at Gyoer to Budapest.

At present, only 63 of the Gysev's total trackage of 217 km are in Austrian territory. Most of its employees are Hungarians, but under company rules Hungarians operating trains in Austria must have "a proper command of German." The rules also provide that all linemen, pointsmen, platelayers, signalmen and station personnel on the Austrian section must be Austrian citizens and that Hungarian train crews must follow directions by Austrian traffic controllers.

The international character of the Gysev has not brought about any unusual difficulties, and train crews from the two countries work together smoothly. The only out-of-the-ordinary aspect occurs on the Gysev's Neusiedl–Pamhagen branch line. There, the rolling stock which has been carrying passengers between the two Austrian towns throughout the day returns empty across the border every evening to spend the night on Hungarian territory.

But that is a minor difficulty compared to some of the line's earlier problems. For instance, in 1891, the Gysev introduced "Middle European time" throughout its lines. "Middle European" or "Budapest time" was 18 min ahead of "Prague time" used in the Austrian parts of the dual monarchy. As a result, passengers arriving at Ebenfurth from Vienna on other lines found that, according to the time tables, their connections on the Gysev had already left 10 or 15 min previously!

RIGHT: A 2-8-0, No 403.607, of the Gysev Railway seen here at Sopron in May 1963. [D. Trevor Rowe

Way out
Private
S763

An electric miscellany

LEFT: Conversation piece at Gatwick Airport on August 22, 1970. In the background can just be discerned the "Brighton Belle" passing at speed. [P. R. Foster

ABOVE: A visitor to the LMR Euston—Watford line on November 4, 1970 was an SR third rail 4COR corridor unit working an LCGB enthusiasts' special from Victoria. It is seen at Watford Junction alongside LMR units, which had then recently been converted from four rail to three rail working. [G. S. Cocks

BELOW: Another view of Gatwick Airport on June 5, 1970 with 2HAP unit No 6049 leading an eight car train which has just arrived from Victoria. The rear four coaches will be detached and the front four will continue to Bognor Regis. [Michael Baker

Platform
11
Platform
10
COVENTRY
Train for
Coventry
departs
1310
calling at
1H42

TOP LEFT: Euston in the off-peak period with an AM10 unit waiting to leave for Coventry on July 21, 1970. [P. R. Foster

BOTTOM LEFT: Class 86 Bo-Bo electric locomotive No E3106 heads the 16.00 Euston—Manchester over the site of Bushey water troughs on August 28, 1970. [J. H. Cooper-Smith

BELOW: Interlude at New Cross Gate with a District Line train about to leave for Whitechapel. [Michael Baker

AN ELECTRIC MISCELLANY
continued

ABOVE: SR 4SUB unit No 4647 arrives at Mitcham Junction bound for Victoria and passes a sister unit standing in the down platform on August 1, 1970.
[P. R. Foster

LEFT: SR 4EPB unit No 5388 stands at Wimbledon on August 1, 1970, bound for London Bridge via Sutton.
[P. R. Foster

AN ELECTRIC MISCELLANY

concluded

ABOVE: a six car electric multiple-unit train runs along the south bank of the Clyde, opposite Dumbarton, on a Glasgow—Gourock working in the summer of 1970. [Derek Cross

RIGHT: One of the former Metropolitan electric locomotives, No 1, *John Lyon*, seen here at Neasden in April 1967; it is a possible candidate for preservation. [A. A. G. Delicata

BELOW: Class 85 electric locomotive No E3085 arrives at Crewe with an express from Euston on July 22, 1970. On the left, Class 86 No E3165 waits to take over a London-bound train. [Derek Cross

Cannon Street, London in the years before the first world war with two SECR Class D 4-4-0s Nos 736 and 737 in the station. Many enthusiasts regard Wainwright's Class D 4-4-0 as one of the most graceful designs ever built.
[From a painting by J. L. Chapman

Some aspects of locomotive aesthetics

JOHN A. LINES

ART, LIKE LOVE, is where you find it, and sometimes it appears in the most unexpected places; for not all good design is to be found in art galleries and it is possible to apply the criteria of artistic judgement to many objects which would not normally qualify as works of art. Among these the British steam locomotive has a strong claim to be included.

Good proportion, an overall impression of unity, a sense of order, clarity of expression, neatness and sensitivity in the treatment of detail are among the chief attributes of all good design. Of these, the first is of fundamental importance, for nothing can redeem a disproportionate piece of design. Moreover, the general proportions of an engine are responsible for its essential character. They give to a bogie engine its sphynx-like dignity; to most 2-4-0s their eager, thrusting-forward look; to a "Paddlebox" or "High Flyer" its apparent top-heaviness; to the typical Holden locomotive its "hunched-up" appearance; and to a Great Western Duke its almost comically exaggerated stateliness. Such descriptions, however, tend to be purely subjective for there are no universally accepted rules of proportion which can be applied to locomotive design. In fact, there are none in any other field of design despite the formulations of distinguished artists and architects from the times of the ancient Greeks to Leonardo da Vinci and le Corbusier. Therefore, in the absence of established criteria, it would seem prudent to leave the question of proportion and pass on to some of the remaining attributes of good design.

If it is accepted that unity, order, clarity, economy and sensitivity are qualities as desirable in the appearance of railway engines as they are in a work of art, then it is possible to adopt an incontravertibly factual and objective approach to locomotive aesthetics. Accordingly, the critical comments which follow are concerned almost exclusively with the means by which locomotive engineers have contrived to weld the various parts of their machines into satisfyingly unified and ordered compositions. Brief comment is made on other aspects of design—felicitous touches or defects in detail—as occasion demands. Even this task is undertaken with trepidation, for sentimental attachments and company loyalties are so strong that to pass judgement on the appearance of a locomotive invariably raises a hornet's nest about the head of the critic!

It seems natural to regard the running plate as a datum-line in describing a locomotive. Like the hem-line, the height of the running plate has tended to rise with the passing of the years. Above this line everything is decently clad and covered over; below it the moving parts are left unencumbered and open to inspection. On a typical Drummond or McIntosh engine the horizontal running plate provided a firm base line which it shared with the tender. Being common to both, it imparted a strong sense of unity and order to the ensemble.

The treatment of the running plate by other engineers is a study in itself. The flowing curves of the type used by Stirling in his famous No 1 were perpetuated by Ivatt and Gresley in their Atlantics and Pacifics. In the Stirling and Ivatt locomotives the smooth flow of line was interrupted by the cylinders and it is interesting to observe how the problem was tackled by the Brighton when that company came to build its Atlantics. The perfect solution was found when the second series, the H2 class, was brought out. Here the running plate rises smoothly over the cylinders to fall again in equally graceful curves

LEFT: The unique Caledonian 4-2-2 No 123, at one time used as royal train pilot and now preserved.
[Locomotive Publishing Company

beneath the firebox—one continuous line. (It is worth noting, in passing, that the rear splashers of the Brighton locomotive were not deformed by the close proximity of the firebox as in the Great Northern version). The line of the running plate designed by Gresley for his Pacifics had all the beauty of a well-shaped melody; a sharp rise from the buffer beam—set against the graceful counterpoint of the main frames—followed by a gentle rise to clear the cranks and a sweeping descent beneath the firebox. When Thompson and Peppercorn altered the classic Gresley design they either broke the line of the running plate where it meets the cylinders—a sad regression—or introduced into it an angularity that was utterly foreign to the original conception. One cannot help observing that a combination of styles frequently proved as distressing in its effects on locomotive design as mixing one's drinks has on the digestion.

To be satisfactory a work of art must possess unity of style. Johnson's designs for the Midland were admirably homogeneous but when rebuilt by Deeley the result was almost always incongruous. Johnson's manner was sauve and elegant, full of graceful curves; Deeley's was more abrupt, angular and chunky. This is not to say that Deeley's own engines were not themselves neat and handsome;

LEFT: Caledonian 4-6-0 No 50 *Sir James Thompson*, a classic among the inside cylinder 4-6-0s of the Edwardian era.
[Locomotive Publishing Company

RIGHT: North Eastern 4-2-2 No 1522.
[Locomotive Publishing Company

it was the mixture of styles that brought disharmony. No less havoc was wreaked on Drummond's graceful engines when they were rebuilt by that austere functionalist Robert Urie. Whatever may be said of Bulleid's notorious U1 0-6-0s it must be admitted that at least they possessed a notable integrity of style.

The point where lack of unity is most likely to appear is obviously at the junction between the engine and tender. The continuing line of the running plate has been cited as a useful visual link between the two. As an additional link the side sheets of the tender were frequently dropped at the front to match the cab opening. In the case of the Midland Decapod and some of the S&DJR 2-8-0s this device found its most complete expression: a canopy was formed at the leading end of the tender which exactly mirrored the contours of the cab opening, making the engine and tender effectively "belong" to each other. In a similar, but less obvious manner, the top of the tender of many streamlined engines was designed to blend harmoniously with the cab roof.

Streamlining itself often had a unifying effect on a locomotive's appearance. Stanier's Coronation Pacifics were amongst the finest of the kind built between the wars. The whole locomotive was contained within one extremely simple, bullet-shaped cowl, decorated with

RIGHT: North Eastern 4-4-0 No 1927, an example of a type with the splashers combined as one unit.
[Locomotive Publishing Company

horizontal stripes which continued along the entire train of the Coronation Scot, adding their own bond of unity to the ensemble. This simple embellishment, which sprung from a V at the front of the engine, was obviously a product of the thirties but it was remarkably restrained in comparison with the vulgar jazz–modern decorations typical of the period. The external casing of the cab and tender in Bulleid's Pacifics followed the contours of the coaches making the whole train appear to be "all of a piece". The fact that the reasons for adopting this shape were practical rather than aesthetic is a feather in the cap of the functionalist who holds that beauty is a natural concommitant of efficiency.

The GWR made a rather half-hearted attempt to jump on the band wagon when the vogue for streamlining was at its height. Only the treatment of the splashers is of interest here as it united the tops of the driving wheels under a single continuous splasher, a practice which had for many years found favour on the LNWR, GCR and NER. The form evolved by T. W. Worsdell for his four-coupled locomotives was extremely bold and served the additional purpose of hiding from sight the Westinghouse pump, a piece of equipment impossible to integrate into the general composition.

The idea of using a continuous flowing line to encompass, and thereby unite, a number of separate elements seems to have occurred as readily to engineers such as Johnson, Wainwright and Robinson as it did to a great artist like Botticelli. All three locomotive men frequently used it to link the splashers of their four-coupled engines. A further refinement was applied to the D and Sir Alexander Class 4-4-0s of the SE & CR and GCR in that the lower portion of the cab swept forwards to meet the rear splashers, forming with them a beautifully unified composition.

The practice of uniting essentially disparate elements simply by merging them together found frequent application on British railways. Splashers would often be merged with the cab or running plate by small transitional curves. An extraneous feature such as a sandbox might similarly be integrated with the adjacent splasher as in Worsdell's class J singles for the NER or in the preserved Caledonian No 123. It is a pity that Stirling was unable to apply a similar treatment to his 8 ft singles for here the sandboxes appeared as unwelcome and unrelated additions to the basic conception.

McIntosh's *Sir James Thompson* for the Caledonian Railway was marred a little by the lettering on the tender which was so large as to be out of scale. Otherwise this splendid design represented a tour de force not only in the application of principles already described but also in the extensive adoption of axial design. All railway engines, when viewed head on, presented a symmetrical appearance; the parts were regularly disposed about a central axis. In the case of this locomotive, however, the principle was extended to the side elevation. A vertical line drawn through the chimney coincided with the centre of the bogie truck, while a second axis passed through the dome and the centre of the leading pair of driving wheels. Admittedly, the former condition is encountered in many bogie engines but the latter is comparatively rare, Johnson's 4-2-2 *Princess of Wales* being probably the most celebrated example. To bring elements in line like this does not always have happy results, however. It gave to Patrick Stirling's inside cylinder singles a curious impression of rigidity where the leading wheels are set on the same axis as the chimney. Though not an example of axial design, it may not be out of place to mention in this context the manner in which Johnson and Stroudley brought the boiler mountings and cabs of their locomotives into subtle relationship with each other by arranging them in such a way that an imaginary straight line could be drawn through the top of each.

The fixing of the handrail on a level with the centre line of the boiler could give a certain aesthetic satisfaction and, for the tidy minded, the pleasure was heightened if it could further be observed that the designer had contrived to hide the vacuum ejector-pipe behind the handrail in the manner adopted by the LNWR.

Nothing is more disruptive to the unified appearance of a locomotive than a disordered array of pipes and gadgets distracting the eye from the basic form. Fortunately British engineers were too well bred to attempt to blind with science the eye of the public!

It is also worth observing how discreet British engineers were in applying (or allowing to be applied) decoration to their locomotives. It is a generally accepted rule of good design that the proper way to apply decoration is to confine it to focal areas in a way that emphasises and helps to define the main features of the composition. In bad design the reverse is the case: the eye is drawn to the decoration itself at the expense of the object it was intended to adorn. For this reason engines bedecked for festive occasions generally looked infinitely less pleasing than they would had they been left unadorned. When the railways were at their most prosperous it was possible to see plenty of decoration of the right kind: chimneys finished with copper caps, brass dome coverings, smoke-boxes adorned with stars at their centres and splashers embellished with brass beading and, in some cases, with name plates.

Probably the best name plates were those applied to the locomotives of the GWR. A properly trained artist takes pains to prepare the eye for the significant features in his design. Whoever was responsible for perpetuating as a standard for all classes the pattern of name plate evolved to suit the old outside

Design from the 1930s is represented by the LMS streamlined *Coronation Scot*; the speed lines along the locomotive were continued on the sides of the coaches.

framed locomotives may have been aware of this fact because the name plate was not just stuck on to the splasher, it was lifted by a distance piece which clearly separated it from the splasher, giving it importance and an identity of its own. The lettering was also especially fine, robust yet distinguished.

A cardinal rule of design is to avoid what is called an unresolved duality. This is a condition where the eye's attention is divided between two objects of equal importance. The problem can be resolved by the introduction of a third object which may be regarded either as a link between the other two or as a pivot about which they seem to balance. Perhaps this is why Stanier provided a dummy dome on his first locomotive for the LMS; he may have been sensitive to the lack of this third element between the chimney and the cab. Certainly many people feel that something was missing on the typical domeless Stirling locomotive, although in the case of his 8 ft singles the driving wheels are so arresting as to make the eye forget any competition between the front and rear of the engine.

Tank engines, by virtue of being self-contained, possessed an inherent unity. The tanks, cab and bunker were usually formed as a continuous whole. The magnificent Baltic tank engines of the Brighton were constructed in this manner, but Stroudley had earlier initiated a much less satisfactory arrangement in which the tanks appeared as separate elements having a greater width than the rest of the superstructure. This may have been an honest expression of function but it did produce an undesirable effect of disunity. Stroudley's practice was followed by Robert Billinton, his successor on the Brighton, but Marsh introduced a more unified arrangement in his Atlantic and Pacific tank engines. In these locomotives the tanks and the bunker were of identical width and rose to the same height; they "lined through", to use an architectural expression. The fact that the handrail on the smoke box door was fixed at the same level as those at the sides of the boiler is a small point but it also contributed to the unified and orderly appearance of the Pacific tanks. This is not to mention the gracefully

A broadside view of SECR Class D 4-4-0 No 740 It is a pity that the black and white reproduction does not do full justice to the elaborate ornamentation.
[Locomotive Publishing Company

curved platform and extended main frames, the neatly contrived smokebox saddle and the shapely chimney. The artistry shown in the design of these superb machines is worthy of close study by any student of aesthetics.

In conclusion it might be an interesting exercise to reconstruct in the imagination some of the processes involved in the design of a locomotive. Imagine, for instance, J. G. Robinson of the GCR supervising the evolution of his beautiful 4-6-0 *Immingham*. Suppose the basic mechanical form has been established and only the finished appearance remains to be determined. It can be assumed that the standard GCR cab, tender and boiler mountings will be used, leaving the treatment of the splashers and running plate to be settled.

He decides to lift the running plate clear of the outside cylinders and to provide separate splashers for the driving wheels. This presents a tricky problem at the rear end of the engine where the cab and rear splashers meet and where the running plate must be dropped again if it is to line through with the tender.

As a first step the splashers and the cab are made the same width, thus enabling the top of the rear splasher to be merged with the cab by use of a small linking curve; the beading of the splasher can then be continued as an arc across the side of the cab until it meets the running plate. This is seen to be the ideal point at which to drop the latter. The curve given to the running plate forms a continuation of the curve of the beading but in the reverse direction and a perfectly smooth transition is achieved. This same curve is now transferred to the front of the engine where the running plate rises to clear the cylinders and is found to coincide nicely with the slope of the main frames.

Described thus the operation seems transparently simple; it was in fact a brilliant solution to the aesthetic problems involved. If anyone doubts it let him start from scratch and devise an alternative arrangement which will as gracefully and naturally unite so many bits and pieces into a unified composition!

Design and its effect on BR stock

MICHAEL BAKER

WHEN DISCUSSING the design of British Rail rolling stock over the past 22 years one must inevitably take into account the work of the Design Panel. One might ask why the engineers cannot be allowed to get on with their work without being pestered by long haired wierdies in pink shirts and fur coats insisting they paint their engines luminous purple and smooth out all the nuts and bolts lest they give the crews a complex. It isn't quite like that actually; the Panel is a highly august body composed mostly of middle-aged gentlemen with a lifetime's experience on the railways behind them. Nevertheless it is not something one could have envisaged having much effect in the days of Francis Webb and Dugald Drummond. It could be argued that each of the major pre-Grouping companies possessed an individuality which was expressed very clearly in visual terms, in the shape and livery of its locomotives and carriages as well as in such architectural features as stations, signal boxes, bridges and so on. Why then should British Railways have found it necessary to employ artists and designers to do something which in days gone by just seemed to happen naturally?

In the first place it never really was like that. One has only to reflect on the importance which has always been paid to distinctive and eye-catching liveries and to thumb through old magazine advertisements and picture postcards issued by the railways to realise that they have always conciously tried to project an image. Until the establishment of the motor car as an everyday means of travel, an event which roughly coincided with the 1923 grouping, the railways of Great Britain had only themselves to compete with, but that could be cut-throat enough. Their position was analogous in some ways with the international airlines of to-day and no-one should need reminding of the vast sums of money they spend on publicity. Similarly there was a certain status attached to someone who worked on the railway. At the top was the engine driver, just as today the airline pilot is considered a rather glamorous character, and even the humblest porter was socially superior to most other manual workers.

By the mid 1950s the position was very different. The railways were a contracting industry, the butt of radio and TV comedians, constantly maligned in the press, a poor third to the airliner and the motor car. Those of us who felt that rail travel had a future knew that a great deal of the criticism was unfair, and if our particular interest happened to be the quaint, the curious and the traditional we were happy enough with the situation as it was. But if the railways had to depend solely on the enthusiast for their income they would go broke overnight. Modernisation had to come and one of the most effective ways of demonstrating to the fare-paying public that there was going to be a change for the better was to up-date and unify the look of British Railways. Hence the setting up in 1956 of the Design Panel.

I am sure the Panel itself would not claim complete success in every field, but it has broadly achieved its primary aim of giving British Rail a distinct and clearly recognisable image. It extends right through from such apparently minor items as letter headings and hat badges to the overall appearance of stations, ships and carriages: but not locomotives. There is no style which may be said to be the hallmark of a British Rail diesel or electric locomotive in the way that there was with steam, whether it be the Swindon one which persisted foi a hundred years or that of British Railways own standards which were in production for only a decade, but were still instantly recognisable as members of one family.

One may feel that the less each type of diesel or electric resembles another the better for the sake of variety, but one can take this attitude too far and finish up with an almost completely unrelated bunch of designs. A criticism often levelled at the one section of British Rail which does present a unified image, the Euston to Birmingham, Manchester and Liverpool electric line is that all the trains are worked by virtually similar locomotives. This is like saying that there was really no difference between a Duchess, a Princess Royal, a rebuilt Scot, a Jubilee, a Class 5 and an 8F. We know that of course there was, but certainly there was a very definite family likeness shared by all these classes and I've never heard any steam enthusiast suggest that it should have been otherwise. So it is with the electric locomotives. The variations in the placing of a grille or the angle of a cab window, let alone the less visible but faı more important differences in mechanical and electrical equipment and power output are just as significant as the size of the boiler or the addition or deletion of smoke deflectors on a steam engine.

Let us see what happens when we venture beyond the present northern limits of the North Western electrified lines. At Crewe our electric locomotive departs and in its place will come an English Electric Type 4 diesel of either the 40 or the 50 class or a Brush class 47. All three are in the same power group and originated on British Railways and yet vary enormously in appearance. We might see other varieties of type 4s at Crewe, for example Swindon Warships or Westerns, and if our journey takes us as far as Carlisle yet another, a Peak; three more British Railways designed locomotives, three more variations in appearance. This is to say nothing of the various type 1s, 2s, 3s and 5s and the four and six wheeled shunters. One might draw a parallel with the early days of steam on a railway like the LB&SCR where practically the only similarity between each engine was its livery.

There are two principal reasons for this situation. One is the indecent haste with which British Railways applied dieselisation,

ABOVE: Examples of BR design showing two standard coaches of the 1950s and a Cravens diesel multiple unit car at the far end. [Michael Baker

permitting each manufacturer, whether an outside one or one of the railway's own workshops, to perpetuate its own designs, the other the Design Panel's failure, when it was belatedly called in, to give the job of shaping the bodywork of all British Railways locomotives to one designer.

Exactly the same thing happened with the diesel multiple units. While locomotive-hauled carriages kept rigidly to very precise specifications multiple-unit vehicles blossomed forth in a plethora of bodywork styles and interior appointments.

A similar situation occurred with colour schemes and emblems. Basically corridor coaches, after initial experiments with the rather pleasing plum and spilt milk were painted red and cream which in 1956 was replaced by what was virtually the old LMS maroon. Multiple-unit vehicles, whether electric or diesel were green and non-corridor locomotive-hauled coaches were at first in unlined red and then lined maroon like the corridor stock. There were however so many variations that it became almost impossible to discover what was the basic one. A great many former Southern Railway locomotive-hauled carriages were never repainted red and cream, and after 1956 all carriages on the Southern Region became green again. At the same time another pre-Nationalisation livery was revived, Great Western chocolate and cream. It was applied only to named expresses on the Western Region, of which there was suddenly a marked increase, and resulted in the somewhat farcial situation of trains running on the same route at identical schedules made up of identical stock but in different colours. Why, if the intention was to emphasise regional differences, all WR passenger vehicles couldn't have been painted chocolate and cream is a bit of a mystery. Chocolate

BELOW: An LMR AL6 with a Liverpool—Euston train passes withdrawn Britannia Pacific No 70024 at Speke in April 1968. [Michael Baker

LEFT: The uninspiring front end of BR electric multiple-units shows little improvement over earlier designs and can be traced back to early Southern practice. This Watford line multiple-unit is entering Euston in June 1969. [Michael Baker

LEFT: The BR diesel multiple unit fleet showed considerable variation in style with designs emanating from various manufacturers. This is a unit built in 1957 by Park Royal, on a Shrewsbury—Crewe working in 1958. [Michael Baker

BELOW: the post-war version of the SR 2HAL unit for semi-fast work was very similar in design to the standard suburban units and the front end can be compared with the Euston—Watford set depicted above. [Michael Baker

and cream was also the livery of Pullman cars, and in 1960 came yet another variation, the blue multiple-unit diesel-electric Pullmans. There seemed little logic behind all this tinkering around with the spectrum, it was partly based on regional differences but only up to a point, for there was no variation in the liveries worn by locomotive-hauled coaches working on the Eastern, Scottish and London Midland Regions although each had its own colour for station nameboards and signs. Yet a Trans-Pennine express, because it happened to be powered by motors placed under the carriages instead of in a separate locomotive, a matter of supreme indifference to a very large proportion of its passengers, was painted green instead of red.

Likewise the locomotive scene grew curiouser and curiouser. It was only natural that in the first few months of Nationalisation there should be a great many variations in the styles of lettering and numbering and in colours, but even after the standard schemes had been decided upon although uniformity sometimes appeared to be on the threshold of attainment it was never quite achieved. Some 7P engines, the A3s for example, were painted blue, others, like the Castles, weren't. Some works were more generous in applying lining to black engines than others, and after a while Swindon apparently found an enormous stock of Brunswick Green or Middle Chrome green, call it what you will, which it had forgotten about since 1948 and started to slap it on everything from Pannier tanks and Standard 4-6-0s to Gas Turbines. The LMS Pacifics changed colour practically every time they visited Crewe and only the Southern, which was anyhow more interested in multiple-units, remained fairly consistent. The Merchant Navys were originally blue before becoming green and sometime later most of the Schools were upgraded from black to the latter colour, incidentally the only 4-4-0s on British Railways to be so dignified. Otherwise all its steam classes bore the same livery throughout the 1950s and until their demise.

Gradually as the Design Panel's influence has taken effect order has been established. One overall livery suffices for every carriage (however it happens to be powered) used on express workings, and another for all those used on stopping trains. The only exceptions to this rule, quite logically, are the Pullmans. There is just one livery for locomotive stock, although there are a number of locomotives which still bear the former green or maroon and this may persist for a little while yet, and British Rail has at last settled on one symbol which is suitable for all occasions.

There is not much which can be done about the differing shapes of the locomotives. We can however take a look at them and see if there are any marks of similarity between the various types, and consider which are the most successful. Everyone has their own view of what is a handsome locomotive and I apologise if I say something nasty about someone's favourite, as I fear I am bound to do.

Let me state first of all that I consider the standard steam engines a most attractive breed. The Britannias were quite the equal of any other class of British Pacific, I can think of no better looking tank engine than the 2-6-4s; the Class 5 4-6-0s were just that little bit more elegant than their immediate predecessors, the Stanier 5s, the Halls and the B1s, and even the Crosti boilered 9Fs had a rather splendidly Germanic air of massiveness about them. Of course they have now gone from British Rail and were the end of a tradition rather than the beginning of one. It is the diesels which in years to come are going to be looked upon as the pioneers.

A feature of American main line diesels had been the nose protruding forward of the cab and it was not perhaps surprising that the earliest British designs, the LMS 10000 and 10001 and then the BR pilot scheme prototypes of 1958/9 should perpetuate this in one form or another, although curiously the three Southern 1Co–Co1s of 1951/4 did not. It was not a feature which by any means necessarily resulted in an unpleasant looking machine, but it did restrict the designer, and by limiting the size of the cab windows prevented him from making full use of what is from an engineman's point of view one of the chief advantages of the diesel and electric over the steam engine.

No 10000 was produced jointly by English Electric and Derby. The 1958 Class 40 D200s came from English Electric, the 1959 Class 44/5/6 Peaks from Derby and both were recognisable descendants of the original main-line diesel. All three designs were of a massive and not unpleasing appearance and it was a style which was perpetuated in three more English Electric types, successfully in the type 3s and the Deltics, not so happily in the smallest of the range the type 2s. The type 1s had a single cab and were more closely related to similar powered locomotives than their bigger brothers. The newest English Electric design, the Class 50 type 4 is quite different again, although it does in fact follow a tradition in that it is the work of the consultant designers Wilkes and Ashmore. The latter had had a hand in a number of BR diesels, sometimes rather disastrously as in the case of the highly over stylised Class 35 Hymeks, on other occasions merely managing to produce something boring like the Birmingham Sulzer type 2s and 3s, sometimes with a fair amount of success, the Brush Class 47 type 4s for example and in at least two instances very happily, in the Deltics and the Class 50s. The one man who seems to have an absolutely sure feel for diesel and electric locomotive design is Professor Mischa Black of the Design Research Unit and one can only regret that the Design Panel did not hand over the entire responsibility for the look of British Rail's locomotives to him.

The first locomotive Mischa Black worked on was the Southern 2,500 hp Bo-Bo electric of 1958, an extremely compact looking design with none of the fussy detail which marred the three earlier Southern electrics and the Manchester–Sheffield EM1s and EM2s. Then came the Swindon Warships and their successors, the Westerns, and the whole family of electric locomotives for the Euston to Liver-

BELOW: Contrast in BR diesel locomotive front ends with, on the left, the Western Class 52 which shows the hand of the BR industrial design team, centre, the BR/Sulzer type 4 a hefty impressive design but with a nose, and, right the Deltic Class 55 with its pronounced nose in front of the driver's cab.

pool and Manchester scheme. I spoke recently to Professor Black about some of his designs.

No locomotive designer can expect to have a completely free hand and the Warships inevitably reflect something of the German diesel-hydraulics from which they were derived. Likewise compromises had to be made with the London Midland electrics. It had originally been decided, and it must be remembered that the first of them came out some twelve years ago, although it hardly seems it, that they should carry a headcode panel placed centrally between the cab windows as had been the practice of the Southern for some 30 years. At a fairly late stage this idea was abandoned but it would have been too costly to revise the cab window layout and so all the LM electrics have the windscreen in three sections instead of two as on the Warships and Westerns. It is a relatively insignificant point but indicative of how cost, unexpected technical problems or lack of foresight on someone's part can frustrate a designer's intentions.

The Western's, Professor Black feels, are his most successful locomotives. By the time he had started work on them he and his team "had learnt a great deal about diesel locomotives", they were given a much freer hand than had previously been the case and the result was the best looking diesels possessed by BR. Professor Black met some opposition over the proposed peaked cab roof, one of the most striking features of the Westerns, but after exhaustive wind tunnel tests was able to prove that aerodynamically it would have no effect on performance. Mischa Black and the Design Research Unit were also responsible for the new livery for British Rail rolling stock, the double arrow symbol, and the staff uniforms. I asked Mischa Black about the variety of colours the Westerns have worn; he said that he considered the original maroon "hideous", quite liked the highly unusual desert sand which surprisingly was not as impractical as it might have seemed, but felt that the now standard blue was the most suitable. I wondered if Professor Black had considered reversing the colours of the main line carriage stock and putting blue above the waistrail, and he said he would have liked to have done so but that it would have been too costly to give the lower panels the constant cleaning they would have needed had they been a pale colour. However it had been possible to paint the Pullmans, which get special attention, in this way. Incidentally an interesting point Professor Black made was that he might well have designed different front ends for his locomotives had he known that they were to be painted bright yellow.

One naturally regrets the passing of the multitude of liveries which was once to be seen on Britain's railways and the variety of types of carriages and locomotives, but British Rail is fighting for its life and it simply cannot spare the money to permit special trains to be painted in distinctive liveries and used on one particular service. Every carriage must be utilised to the full and when it becomes out of date and uneconomic to maintain in good running order then it has to go. It would be pleasant to retain in service such vehicles as the ex-"Devon Belle" and "Coronation" observation cars, the best of the pre-war Pullmans, special saloons, restaurant cars and so on, but it would be an expensive indulgence which BR cannot afford. Fortunately the latest Mark II corridor coaches are a great improvement on their predecessors, and the much maligned and sorely pressed Southern Region has at last licked the problem of multiple-units with square wheels and no springs and is now producing some very comfortable if not especially beautiful semi-fast and express stock [even if the internal layout of the Brighton and Portsmouth 4CIG driving trailers is barbaric—ED.]. A revolution in surburban stock is around the corner and if the Glasgow blue trains and the latest London Midland AM10 multiple-units are an indication of the form it is going to take then commuters may find their lot somewhat happier.

Whatever happens, the perceptive enthusiast needn't fear that all individuality will disappear. The diversity of British Rail services is far too great ever for that to happen.

Steam in Germany.....

LEFT UPPER: A DB Class 051 2-10-0 pauses in front of the signal operating room at Rheine. [Keith Lawrence

LEFT LOWER: A sight for sore eyes for British enthusiasts; a group of Class 044 and 050 2-10-0s at Ehrang shed in July 1969. [Judy Wallis

ABOVE: A pair of Class 053 2-10-0s, coupled chimney to chimney, work a hopper train near Meppen on March 28, 1970. [Keith Lawrence

BELOW: Contrast in German steam power is this 0-4-0 tram engine built by Krauss in 1887 and still working on the Chiemseebahn in Bavaria. [Ian G. Holt

48
1

ABOVE: An oil-fired Class 012 Pacific heads a light-weight train from Meppen towards Emden in the summer of 1970. [Keith Lawrence

LEFT: Steam in the Mosel Valley: a Class 044 2-10-0 and a three cylinder 2-10-0 pass with freight trains at Cochem at the entrance to the Cochemer Tunnel, the longest in Germany, in June 1970. [R. A. Hunter

BELOW: The impressive Class 001 Pacific, No 230-2, leaves Hof for Bamburg with an evening express on May 29, 1969. [M. Randall

C.P. 284

ABOVE: Portuguese narrow-gauge 2-6-0T No E92 stands at Celorico de Basto on September 21, 1970 with an Ian Allan special on the line from Livracao.
[Keith Smith

.....and in Portugal

LEFT: Henschel inside-cylinder 4-6-0 No 284 blackens the town of Pinhao with the 06.45 Regua—Pocinho mixed train.

BELOW: Another Portuguese narrow gauge scene with 1911 Henschel-built Mallett 2-4-6-0T No E208 near Vila Real with the 10.21 Regua—Chaves on September 4, 1970.
[A. G. Cattle

Corner seat to the Orient

C. PORTWAY

WHENEVER I had reason to mention that in March I was visiting my cousin in Beirut I invariably provoked a stock reply.

"How pleasant. You're going by air of course."

It wasn't even framed as a question. Unless I was simply calling there as part of a Mediterranean cruise the aeroplane was taken as the only logical mode of travel to a Middle-Eastern destination 4,000 miles away.

"No, I'm going by train."

Again the reaction was predictable. "Train!" came the exclamation. "Good heavens, *can* you get there by train?" Then as the implications sunk in a certain whimsical fascination crept into the final remark. "You know it could be quite fun."

It was the understatement of the year.

With but a month at my disposal I had of course investigated the more obvious means of reaching the Lebanon. Like the sore thumb the offerings of the world's airlines stood out a mile, even screaming it from the hoardings on the A4 around Heathrow. BEA did it, Air France did it, Middle East Airlines did it, BOAC loftily condescended to do it on the way to somewhere else and the Communist MALEV did it via Budapest cheaper than anyone else. It was all too easy, too fast and I didn't think my cousin could stand me for a whole month.

I looked at the shipping lines but these were expensive and excrutiatingly slow. Furthermore the social life was not for me; nor were those short stops at the more exotic Mediterranean ports which smacked too much of snatching carrots away from a donkey.

So I turned to the overland possibilities as I knew I would. A formidable but fascinating assortment of countries stood at my feet. France, Switzerland, Italy, Yugoslavia, Bulgaria, Greece, Turkey, Syria and the Lebanon. The railway had it from the start. The Eurobus lines did not become effective until late April

LEFT: Until a few years ago the first stage of a journey by rail to the Orient on the European mainland would have been from Calais to Paris with an SNCF Pacific; No 231 E 40 heads the 14.45 Calais Maritime—Paris near St Josse in September 1963. [J. C. Beckett

and the local bus services, though no doubt a delightful means of transportation, were too erratic a method for the time at my command. No, the railway it would be and there was an added bonus in that the Turkish State Railway, who would convey me about four thousand miles of the round trip, was amongst the cheapest in the world.

There was only one snag and this temporary but it affected me. Syria, for political reasons, was allowing no British or American travellers through her territory. She was biting her own nose but it did add a complication as it would mean flying between Adana in Southern Turkey and Beirut. I tried various ruses to get a visa from the Syrian Embassy but they wouldn't play. However, it was a short hop and not an expensive one.

Clutching a volume of second class rail tickets I descended upon Victoria station. Recent snow had finally thawed but it was still cold. I went in search of a warm lunch.

Baked Beans, Fried Egg & Toast, Two Sausages & Bacon, (accent on the two), Grilled Ham, Grilled Bacon, Pizza, Steak Pie, Ham Omelette, Plain Ditto!

So read the menu in the strategically situated express restaurant with a well-known name tag. The pizza struck a discordant note but I applauded the gesture to internationalism. I stopped applauding when I saw it. I ordered grilled ham with an egg and tomatoes.

"It's off," I was told with a glance at the clock which said twenty-five to two or, in the parlance of Victoria station, 13.35.

"What's on?" I asked resignedly.

I knew what was coming. "There's the pizza," the waiter said. I glanced again at the dried-up replica of that Italian institution *from which portions were being cut like a cake.* "Perhaps you can rustle me up some chips with an egg or something," I suggested hurriedly.

The dispenser of Anglo-Italian delicacies moved away. At least he didn't actually *say* that 13.35 was past his or anyone else's lunchtime.

Clearing a space on a table strewn with the debris of earlier and more considerate diners I consumed my soggy, luke-warm fare. A poster above me extolled the virtues of the Italian capital. I made a date to have my pizza in Rome on the way home.

Much has been written about Victoria Station. The gateway to the Continent British Rail likes to call it. Others, less kindly, say: "Abandon hope all ye that enter here." It is one of the oldest, certainly the draughtiest stations in London. It's been despatching and receiving continental trains for a century but the chaos remains. Nobody knows anything. Nobody *wants* to know anything. And when some bright spirit does volunteer a snippet of information or inspired guess it's certain to be contradicted a moment later. Men in blue frock coats and the magic words "Wagons-Lit Cook" on their hats frown at their time pieces and cockney porters crack doubtful jokes in loud highpitched voices across the platforms. Train destination boards at the head of the platforms look like Dick Whittington sign-posts, the customs shed on platform 8 a cattle market and the continental ticket and enquiry office, way across the street, looks like nothing at all because nobody can find it. All this was before the new family-sized departure indicator was built.

Miraculously my 15.30 slid out of this morass of disorganisation at half-past three on the dot. But in the last minutes my jaundiced view of Victoria Station had been softened. Just before the whistles blew I watched a porter trundle an old man in a wheelchair down the platform to the luggage van. Beside him his wife, obviously foreign, scuttled along searching desperately in her handbag for a suitable tip. The cripple safely stowed the porter stemmed the flow of French gratitude and gently snapped shut the old woman's bag.

"That's all right, love," he said grinning, "You keep it to make your hubby better," and with that he walked away.

Victoria station can have my custom any day.

It would be an event if there had been no chaos either at Folkestone or Dover but to fight one's way onto the Channel steamer has become part of the English way of life. They still part the sheep from the goats, though the heading "Foreign Passports" has given way to the softer "Non-British Passports". A Treasury official looked me hard in the eye and asked if I was taking more than my currency allowance out of the country. I told the truth when I said I wasn't but would have been happy to have sunk to the level of a "Foreign Passport" on that score.

Ever since my first Hornby train set railways have never ceased to hold a certain fascination for me. I know little about the technical side of railways or rolling stock and whether a locomotive is a Pacific 4-6-2 or a Diesel-hydraulic 2000 hp leaves me cold. Frequent commuting between Essex and Liverpool Street on what is surely the most uncomfortable and uninspiring train service in Europe does its best to knock interest out of me though in recent years I have fulfilled lifelong ambitions to drive both a surface and an underground train. Transworld expresses have also formed an, as yet, unrequited passion, with the Orient Express well to the fore.

To the completely uninitiated it ought to be explained that the Orient Express as such no longer exists. The original train ran between Calais and the Rumanian port of Constanza (with a branch to Varna). These days there are a number of expresses running over various routes but all with a common interest in "feeding" the Balkans. There is the Arlberg running between Paris and Bucharest. The Ostend-Vienna, the Berlin-Istanbul serving Prague, Bratislava and Budapest, The Athens Express between Niš in Yugoslavia and the Greek capital, The Tauern Orient from Munich linking with the Direct-Orient from Paris to Belgrade which, in turn becomes the Marmara Express for the onward journey via Sofia to Istanbul.

The train that skulked at a badly lit platform in the Gare de Lyon in Paris was the Direct-Orient Express with through coaches to Athens and Istanbul. It was the one that everybody means by the Orient Express and it left, on time, at the romantic hour of ten minutes before midnight. But there the romance died.

The inaugural trip of the Orient Express in 1883 was a tremendous occasion with many crowned heads of Europe and Asia participating. At its zenith in the early 1900s the great train could accomplish the distance between Paris and Istanbul in 56 hr. Yet now my timetable figures totted up a total of 84! (And I was not to know that it would be two hours late into the bargain!) Only in France can it claim to be an express at all and even here various sections of it hang around the Gares du Nord and de Lyon as if reluctant to leave Paris. With Vallorbe and the Swiss border it becomes a commuters' special stopping at all stations and making a mockery of its proud destination boards bearing such magic names as Paris – Lausanne – Milano – Venezia – Trieste – Zagreb – Beograd – Sofia – Athens – Istanbul.

I remembered the reasons for this dawdling of the Orient Express through both Switzerland and Italy. From Paris there are two departures for Istanbul the other being routed via Munich. The German section takes three hours longer and since a 03.00 departure from Paris was frowned upon as an inconvenient hour for a great express to leave from a great capital the timetable conference delegates agreed to the policy of an idling Swiss–Italian section until the connection of the two portions in Yugoslavia.

The conference also has the task of satisfying all the countries through which the express passes. It was the Yugoslavs who terminated the Simplon-Orient because its schedule meant an arrival in Belgrade in the middle of the night. Like the proposed 03.00 departure from Paris it was killed stone dead though the reason was basically more commercial. Even the name "Simplon Orient", liked by the Bulgarians and Turks, was changed to "Direct-Orient" and for this the Swiss—a big force in the railway world—were responsible. The Yugoslavs kept silent during this controversy. They had what they wanted; the new express gave them a 09.00 arrival in Belgrade.

The rock infested greenness of Switzerland ended with the Simplon tunnel and we came out the other side into a world of powdery white snow. But the pure whiteness soon lost its virginity as the train dropped down to the Lombardy plain and crept for comfort into the great soulless metropolis of Milan, prosperous and commercial, thriving but shivering in a cold drizzle.

Italy had been included in the route of the Orient Express only since 1919. Previously it had passed over the territory of Germany and Austria but these countries had been defeated in the first world war and in the "holier than thou" attitude taken by the Allies at the time of the Treaty of Versailles the idea of a grand Express of international repute crossing the tainted ground was repugnant. Furthermore the Simplon tunnel had recently been opened to traffic between Brig and Domodossola. This development well pleased Italy who was building a gigantic showpiece station at Milan and wanted a showpiece train to grace it. Beyond lay a newly-created Yugoslavia with which France was anxious to establish friendly relations and, supported by the Swiss and the Dutch, the Simplon-Orient Express was born offering sleeping and dining car service right through to Salonika and Athens. Things have deteriorated slightly since then however. In place of a dining car over much of the route is an abomination called a "tray meal service". As we ambled undeterminably towards Venice I found the cold fare to be almost as plastic as the tray that bore it!

Trieste, in contrast to Milan, was having a fortaste of summer and as we entered the dry, sullen landscape the chirping of crickets defied the calendar. In sympathy the sea switched from green to blue.

It was with some trepidation that I watched the train zig-zag up the steep incline to the Yugoslav frontier station of Cezana. Hardly eighteen months had passed since at this very place I had effected the Iron Curtain escape of my Czech brother-in-law. In doing so I had "bent" a number of Yugoslav laws and had cause to wonder whether authority had caught up with me. If so, here was its chance to pounce. A variety of officials passed in and out of the almost empty train but only one took close interest in me. Having burrowed through my stamp-choked passport several times he made close reference to a note-book containing, presumably, a list of undesirables. I waited, my fingers firmly crossed, and though the man combed the pages thoroughly my name, it seemed, was not among the legion of the damned. He looked disappointed. Maybe he'd seen my face before somewhere . . .

There is no room for sentiment in the communist mentality, and though only a light shade of pink, Yugoslavia had to debunk still further the remaining shreds of glory that clung to the Orient Express after its whistle-stop tour of northern Italy. During the long wait at Cezana a number of very local coaches and even a couple of cattle trucks had joined the train. We had sunk to the level of what Germans call a personenzug and had even to play second fiddle to the connection for Rijeka which left before us. I remembered it was the same with the Arlberg Orient in Austria and Hungary some years before. In spite of Russian sanctions Austria had managed to electrify the line between Salzburg and Vienna thus maintaining the standard of a train with the proud full title of the Swiss-Arlberg-Vienna-Orient Express. But what crawled out of the capital's down-at-heel East station was a three coach affair plus a couple of open trucks. Even then everything was searched and prodded with bayonets at the border town of Hegyeshalom before the one-time express was allowed to proceed to Budapest. To only a slightly lesser degree it is a similar story at Cheb on the Czech line to Prague.

From the balmy warmth of Trieste we plunged again into thick snow at Ljubljana. It lay, admittedly thawing, heavy upon the ground and in spite of a switch from electric to steam traction the Yugoslav Federal State Railway deemed it necessary to ration the central heating. I sat shivering in semi-darkness until the blaze of light that was Zagreb.

Almost immediately my compartment was invaded by a squad of young soldiers an arsenal of weapons and implements festooned about them. I gave up three of the four seats along which I had been reclining with little reluctance for it had been too cold for sleep. My new companions eyed me for a few moments discussing my probable nationality amongst themselves. I heard myself labelled German, American, Norwegian and French before the list founded in a welter of Serbo-Croat. At least they had an answer for the lack of heat. A corporal with an india-rubber face produced a lemonade bottle of slivovice and passed it round. Each took a substantial swig the last hesitatingly passing the bottle to me. The fire water bit into my entrails and I said: "Danke schön" and then "Thank you". The corporal was the scholar. "Engleski?" he enquired eager to prove his superior knowledge. I nodded and his face folded into a grin. Forthwith I became an honorary member of the Yugoslav Army. Two more bottles followed the first and the swigs became gulps. We held long incomprehensible conversations in which the occasional word that was universally understood became a signal for celebration and therefore more slivovice. When the heat came on an hour later it didn't really matter for we were all dozing happily on each other's shoulders!

Uninterrupted sleep was effectively denied us however by the repeated incursions into the compartment of the ticket inspector. A thin, lugubrious individual he obviously held a low opinion of the army and smelt a fish regarding the collective travel voucher held by the corporal. For those of us who cared to look, dawn illuminated the most featureless section of the journey so far. Right up to Belgrade, the equally featureless capital, the flooded plain offered a dismal picture of a vast sea of mud. Dotted thinly across the landscape tiny villages, like islands, clung to almost impassable mud roads that were their only link with civilisation.

At Belgrade Central station my military companions departed and my compartment became as empty as their lemonade bottles. Before he left the corporal gave me a wink and I remembered a wartime journey I had made between London and Carlisle on a platform ticket! The train gave me a circular tour of the city, an apparently necessary procedure when transferring from one platform to another, but my impressions of the Yugoslav capital remained unflattering.

The status of my compartment rose however with the entry of an Italian lady and a Yugoslav Airforce officer. They were separate but lost no time in repairing this state of affairs even though both stoutly clung to their mother tongues! The officer wore a superbly creased uniform and a David Niven moustache while the focal point of the lady was, I was soon to learn, a red gash of a mouth clamped permanently round a cigarette. Obviously the uniform meant more than the budding acquaintance to the gallant captain for a tremendous spring cleaning operation was put in motion before the sea-green trousers were allowed contact with the seat. Flicking the sparse furnishings with a lace handkerchief he next covered the seat with sheets of my discarded newspaper upon which I had previously deposited my feet. Various items of outer apparel were then carefully folded and deposited on the newly polished rack before the lesser business of wooing could begin.

From the little snippets of Italian I could understand from the object of his attentions it became obvious that she was no lady. I watched the blue smokescreen ascend in thickening spirals all but obscuring the no-smoking notices, and coughed pointedly. The officer noticed my stare of disapproval and offered me a peppermint. It was the first of many from a bottomless supply.

Whenever he could see his new girl friend through the fog he would lean forward and dash off an ode in Serbo-Croat. She responded with less enthusiasm and eventually it got through to him that she was cold. With enormous chivalry the captain threw caution to the winds and wrapped his overcoat around her knees. I watched his eyes trying to avoid the sight of a sleeve trailing in the dirt of the floor. But it was all in vain. The train rattled into Niš and in Niš lay his duty. Almost despairingly he swept up his coat, threw us each a last peppermint and fled.

Approaching the legendary Dragoman Pass the railway has to bore a way through the northern buttresses of the Balkan Mountains. The pass itself, a winding chasm in which the single track and the flooded tributary of the Nišova river became almost one, was curtained by a blizzard. At Dimitrovgrad the Bulgarian customs had their pound of flesh and by the simple expedient of turning our bags upside down were able to effect their examination. Italian female and British male underwear lay strewn over the seats like a Women's Institute rummage sale.

I was still struggling to close my bag when the train slowed at the suburbs of Sofia. I was to break my journey at the Bulgarian capital and though I had doubts of its likely attractions—doubts built upon experience of other communist shrines—the city seemed worthy of a visit.

Accordingly I bade "Arrivederci" to my companion and for the first time in fifty hours left the train. At first I thought I had made a mistake and alighted at the wrong station so small and rural a place it was. Afterwards I learnt that the original main station had been bombed in the war and nobody apparently had thought to build a new one. Fighting my way through the Saturday night crowd that spilt dangerously over on to the tracks I emerged at a tram terminus.

With no Bulgarian money, lugging a heavy suitcase and with every notice and sign in an incomprehensible script I would have had difficulty in locating the city centre even by public transport. But to have travelled in any direction in these circumstances was an impossibility. Every square inch of tram was occupied inside and out and queues waited at the stops. For me, in spite of the added impediment of a sleet storm, it was a case of "take up thy bed and walk".

Struggling along Georgi Dimitrov street (though the name plates didn't put it as simply as this) because the tram lines looked denser in the direction it led I began to think my reasoning had let me down. I saw nothing that even looked remotely like a hotel but at a restaurant a kind waitress, who spoke a word or two approximating to English, confirmed that, in fact, I was on the right road. She also pressed a tram ticket on me and tried to explain the system by which one purchases tickets—usually in blocks—at kiosks prior to

BELOW: On the Greek State Railways an Alco diesel No A 303 restarts the "Direct Orient" express from Paris to Athens at Titherea after attaching a restaurant car on June 11, 1964. [D. Dixon

boarding the vehicle. An element of trust is involved since you clip your own ticket but should a check uncover a ticketless passenger the penalties are severe. I carried on walking.

Suddenly to my joy I was in Vladimir Iljic Lenin Square—though the "little Father" seldom inspired this emotion in my heart—and straightway found myself in the centre of a gang-fight. Joy switched to alarm as a squad of pistol-wielding policemen waded into the knot of youths into which I had blundered. One of the contestants ran into me and sprawled head first ôver my suitcase with a policeman on top of him. Hastily I retired to safer regions.

My bleats for assistance in locating a hotel (for the Bulgarian script for even so international a word in the brightest neon was Chinese to me!) at first met with no response until, at about the fifth attempt, a group of people abruptly realised that there was an Englishman in their midst. There was almost a rush to claim me. Following much gesticulating and airing of school exercise-book English I was marched off inside a box of Sofian citizens all talking at once.

I had not intended to aim so high as the Grand Hotel into which imposing vestibule we trooped. With my squad of chaperons arrayed behind me I enquired about rooms. Being outside the season there were plenty and upon learning the extremely reasonable price I nearly surrendered without further ado. But I have a stubborn streak and I had heard talk of a private accommodation service that existed in Bulgaria. This would not only be cheaper still but also offer an insight into a Bulgarian home.

My further enquiry led me and my retinue round the corner to the still open offices of "Balkantouriste". "English!" exclaimed the girl clerk slightly taken aback. "I fear we can only offer you a German-speaking host."

"That will do fine," I said with optimistic trust in my extremely limited German and no sooner said than done for there stood my host at my elbow.

I am quite sure that my escort would have come to blows over which of them was to accommodate me had they understood what was going on. As it was, a lot of bewildered muttering ensued as I paid the small service charge and, murdering the German language, my host and I escaped into the street. Even though by changing some money at the agency I was no longer a pauper my new friend insisted upon treating me to a taxi to his home off the broad 9th of September Street.

The two days that followed were full of interest. Being a week-end my host was free and insisted upon giving me the complete Cook's tour of Sofia. I saw the vaults of the Alexander Nevsky Cathedral with its exquisite religious drawings, the nauseating spectacle of Dimitrov's embalmed corpse in its see-through grave, the museum of the revolutionary movement full of rusty machine-guns and fragments of underground newspapers, the Archeology museum, the fascinating church of St. Sophia and the finish of a People's Army long distance relay race at the Liberation memorial where the exhausted runners were supposedly revitalised by the sight of fresh hoardings extolling the unbreakable bond that was Bulgarian–Soviet friendship. One contestant was violently sick at the finishing line but I think it was just exhaustion.

Only once did I bring up politics with my host. I asked him what he thought of his own army marching into Czechoslovakia. He was not the slightest abashed. "The Czechs asked for trouble and got it," he replied. Though he professed not to be a member of the Communist party his sympathy was not at variance with it. I noticed another thing. Sofia was the only Communist capital I knew of late where political slogans were still an accepted part of the landscape. But so were packed churches.

The second evening my hostess joined us for a meal in a Bulgarian folk restaurant that lay in the shadow of Sofia's mountain, Vitosha. It was obviously a popular night-spot and we ate kebab and drank local wine out of mugs shaped like tea-pots while troupes of dancers pranced around to castanets and balalaikas. Next morning I attempted to climb Vitosha as an antidote to the excesses of the previous evening but was defeated by drifts of soft snow.

For our midday meals we patronised the People's "Help Yourself" restaurants that appeared to be a big draw to diners of all walks of life. The food was certainly cheap but exceedingly nasty. Consisting mainly of various types of würst, beans, shredded onions and chips it was served luke-warm on badly washed plates. The beer, in unlabelled bottles, might have been what they washed them in.

For an hors d'oeuvre we frequented a more classy establishment which appeared to specialise in home-baked bread consumed with a "dip" of pepper. Too much of the latter and you blew your head off! Whether or not it was because of the explosive properties of the "dip" but I noticed the waiters going around wearing masks. Hygiene is taken seriously in the larger Bulgarian towns; barbers and food shop assistants invariably wearing masks likewise. Maybe one day the hygiene bug will spread to the People's restaurants.

Struggling with a little-known language does not bode well for prolonged friendship and I think the feeling of relief was mutual when I was seen off on the evening train; the same portion of the Orient Express I had left 48 hr before. The couple had been immeasurably kind by giving me a home from home in their small flat but the call of the open railroad was loud in my ears.

Ensconsed in a corner seat my mind, activated by a kind of built-in thermostat, began sorting out the living habits peculiar to train-travel. Hard experience had given me an insight into the art of sleeping on trains without using wagons-lit. Coaches varied; most second-class compartments catered for a complement of eight: four to each seat with an arm in the middle. Very occasionally it was only six. Out of the tourist season numbers in a compartment seldom exceeded six for long and by spreading oneself or giving an impression that you are holding a seat for a friend it is usually possible to discourage unwanted bodies when mass intrusion threatens. And it is surprising what can be done with a neighbouring empty seat. Padding the hard arm rest in the corner with a jacket or coat for a pillow some degree of comfort can be attained curled up like a cat. Three changes of position can be achieved as soon as cramp sets in and a stretch of the legs can be accomplished upwards over the central head rest. But I was still a novice at these proceedings as the Orient Express shuffled towards the Greek and Turkish borders.

An impressive Russian-built diesel locomotive led us to Plovdiv and then stole away into the night as if ashamed of having soiled itself by hauling a train that brandished such names as PARIS, LAUSANNE and VENICE. Thereafter we were back to steam again.

Until the second city of Bulgaria my travelling companions not only numbered the full complement of seven but were the roughest bunch of cut-throats imaginable. The ticket inspector, on seeing them, raised his eyes to heaven and gave me a pitying glance. Making sure my wallet was close to my skin I prepared for the worst. Soon I was the object of a merciless interrogation but again, upon learning of my nationality, I became exhibit number one and was treated with a deference that accorded to my rarity. It was only the acrid smoke of eight stupefying cigarettes that caused me relief when Plovdiv emptied the compartment.

The builders of the main line out of Bulgaria could hardly be blamed for the convulsions of history that, in the course of a few years made Edirne Russian, Turkish, Bulgarian, Turkish, Greek, and, as it is now, Turkish. Hence the line passes unnecessarily twice through a few dozen miles of Greece and with no love lost between Greeks, Bulgarians and Turks, the Greeks insist upon a long and thorough passport and customs check both going in and coming out of their slices of territory. This is just one expression of a hate that simmers beneath the surface as the three belligerants kick each other under the table and should the innocent traveller suffer it's just too bad. A new line is under construction that will by-pass Greek territory though the odds are that further strife will once more revise the frontiers which will doubtless make it necessary to start the work all over again!

But dawn made amends for the petty quarrelling of man. Creeping up over the low hills came a gorey football of a sun dyeing the barren scrub-covered land in an unnatural orange tint. A profusion of wild snowdrops, crocuses and fluffy tumbleweed gleamed like fireflies through the crimson haze. Even in a state of semi-consciousness I had been able to tell when we were on Greek soil and not Turkish. The lullaby of the wheels had abruptly increased to a rapid tempo—like light infantry on the march—as we passed over short lengths of rail. Laid thus for easy manhandling instead of being welded and placed by tracklayer the remoter areas of Greece are the last strongholds of this old fashioned method of railway construction. My companions—a trio of Yugoslav students—stirred and rose from various contortionist positions of sleep as the train crawled across the rolling downs of European Turkey. My portable electric razor went the rounds for which service I was presented with breakfast gratis.

The first hamlets with their white sentinel minarets speckled the countryside each supplying a quota of waving villagers to welcome a train that went by three times every week of their lives. Their numbers and fervour increased as our panting locomotive hauled us up and over the crest of one of the hills of Istanbul. By midday we had reached the sea and leaving the international airport on our left wound our way beneath the walls of the Topkapi Palace into the last outpost of Europe.

Istanbul. What can one say about this fabled city that nobody has said a thousand times before. But its magic was slow to filter through to me that warm and sunny afternoon. Maybe I was tired but my first impressions as I strolled through the old city of Stambul were cynical and unkind. Take away the mosques and minarets and you have a vast slum stretching across seven hills and divided by an oily waterway. A loud, overcrowded slum hooting and yelling and flaunting its poverty.

And then as I walked the spell was woven and through the dirt and squalor I saw Istanbul in all its magnificence. The magic lies in the people. The slick leather-jacketed traffic police, the Bosphorus ferry captains, the tough untidy soldiers, the voluble vendors of everything under the sun, the orange squeezers, the illegal money changers, the waiters, shop assistants, priests and the vast mosaic of humanity that *is* Istanbul. A city can be the loneliest of places but loneliness is an emotion difficult to attain in the former Turkish capital. For three days I explored its labyrinth of streets on foot and by taxi. It was in Istanbul that I made my acquaintaince with that most practical and economic of transportation the *Dolmus*, a community taxi usually plying a fixed route in or between towns. Wherever I went, friendly smiling citizens, rich and poor, accosted me offering advice and greeting. Even the street vendors had a special quality about them, a transaction being of secondary importance to a complicated conversation with an out-of-season Englishman.

A voyage up the Bosphorus in one of the many ferries hooting its way across the busy straits gave me, for an outlay of little more than a shilling, an insight into the growing spread of Istanbul, its suburbs now almost reaching the Black sea. Uskudar, Galata-Besiktas, the double fortress of Rumeli Hisar and Anadolu Hisar, Beykoz and beyond. The ship's captain came and talked with me and as we sipped small glass beakers of tea I learnt of the respect and trust with which his profession is held throughout Turkey. It was raining when we returned to the ferry terminus by the unimposing Galata Bridge but the magic could not be doused.

The Turkish Railway of Europe and that of Asia are, to all intents and purposes, different rail systems. The Bosphorus ensures that the traveller ends his journey at Istanbul. He can then start another if he so desires but there is no such amenity as a through-carriage, rail ferry or even an attempt at a time-link between the two sections of railway. From Europe your journey ends at Sirkeci Station and that's that. For Asia and the east the journey *starts* at Haydarpasa, a ten-minute Dolmus ride and half an hour by ferry if you time your connection right. In small print Cook's Continental Timetable warns passengers in direct transit via Istanbul to allow up to eight hours for connection between trains. This seemed to me a gross exaggeration. No railway surely could be *that* far out in its schedules.

In spite of my scepticism I reached Haydarpasa Station with nearly two hours to spare. My immediate destination was the town of Adana in southern Turkey beyond the Taurus Mountains. By the Taurus Express the journey was quoted as 30 hours. On the outward trip I had chosen to go via Ankara and return via Konya thus covering a little more of Turkey. My tickets were made out for the other way round which caused an immense amount of form-filling and ticket endorsements. Because I would be doing an extra 250 kilometres on the outward journey I was surcharged four Turkish Lira or about 3s 6d. which didn't strike me as all that scandalous—particularly when the ticket clerk insisted on me sharing a cognac with him in his office!

Statistics show that the present mileage of the Turkish Railway totals 4,976. When compared with, say, Sweden—equally mountainous, considerably smaller and with almost double the track mileage—it will be appreciated that the railway in Turkey is somewhat thin on the ground. But what there is constitutes a considerable engineering feat—(in the Taurus Mountains there are 22 tunnels within just over 30 miles) in spite of the fact that most of the network is single track and non-electrified.

A history of the Turkish Railway becomes a study in politics. Construction of the railway began in 1888, when a German company secured permission to build the Anatolian Railway running from Haydarpasa to Ankara via Eskehir and, later, Konya. Following the state visit to Constantinople by Kaiser Wilhelm II a convention was signed between the two countries granting the German Anatolian Railway an extension to Kuwait, on the Persian Gulf. This was but another concession in support of Germany's *Drang nach Osten*—Drive to the East—that was the frustrated envy of politicians in Britain, France and Russia.

But opinion in Britain at least was divided. Largely out of dislike for France and Russia considerable support was given to the Germans and their plans to push the railway through to Baghdad by way of two routes. One was the old imperial route of the Romans through Angora (Ankara) and Shivas; the other followed the valley of the Meander river and over the enormous bulk of the Taurus Mountains into the plains of Mesopotamia.

The German line had got as far as Basra when the war came in 1914 and four years later Allenby's armies swept through much of the area capturing vast amounts of rolling stock and equipment. Thereafter the dream of economic conquest changes its nationality. But British railway concept was more ambitious still. As well as the link with Baghdad a line south through Beirut, Haifa, and Gaza to Cairo was proposed. By 1930 the Paris–Baghdad route by the Orient and Taurus Expresses was a reality and the time-tables of the years before the second world war involved the whole Eastern European and Middle Eastern complex.

Since then the realisation of the dream has withered with the growth of air travel and the post 1939–45-war situation in the Middle East. Turkey has taken over one by one the lines originally built with European rather than Turkish money and, in support of her more modest dreams, has built lines linking the Anatolian routes with the Black Sea and the Persian frontier. The Cook's Grand Tour for elegant ladies and dashing gentlemen was discreetly dropped from the agency's brochure and the romance of a journey from Paris to Baghdad has become as faded as that of the destination boards on the Taurus coach sides.

Even so I was scandalised by the state of the present day Taurus Express. Never have I seen a filthier train. The compartments were thick with grime and soot, the windows opaque with dirt, the seatless toilets an affront to humanity. The Yugoslav coach on the Orient Express in which I had travelled from Sofia had been nothing to write home about, but the Taurus Express, which included international through coaches to such places as Baghdad, Damascus and Beirut, hit rock bottom. To cap my disgust I had my first dispute with a Turk who demanded the equivalent of 5s for lifting my bag of his own accord onto the train. He got a shilling and a rude Anglo-Saxon instruction. Gingerly I parked myself in the cleanest corner seat I could find, weighed up the position of various head and arm rests, and prepared to endure thirty hours of suffering.

By the time we moved out of the station I had with me in the compartment two Syrian youngsters and a quiet studious-looking Turk. A threatened invasion by three companions of the Syrians with a virtual mountain of luggage I successfully discouraged. I didn't much like the look of the ones I'd got with me and we sat glowering at each other as the suburbs of Istanbul evaporated into isolated villages and small towns.

Between Haydarpasa, Uskudar and Izmit the train made good time giving, outwardly, a reasonable imitation of an international express. The thickly populated plateau followed by the Turkish naval base drew all eyes in the compartment and in the general interest our hostility vanished. Forthwith I became the mascot of the Syrians and, one by one, their companions elsewhere in the train were invited into the compartment for an "interview" Politics, the topical politics of the Arab–Israel conflict, quickly became the chief subject for discussion our exchanges being carried out in a mixture of French and English.

There was no bitterness. For the Syrian Arabs the fact that England was, to them, backing the wrong horse, was simply reason for great sorrow. Nor was there great hate. The Israeli's of course had a right to live in peace. But not by stealing other people's land. I was forcibly reminded of a similar theme of thirty years before. Hitler called it "lebensraum". Stolidly, as if uncomprehending, the studious Turk in the corner listened in silence to the tortuous debate. His countrymen had played it strictly neutral in *that* conflict, too. . .

One cannot travel far in Turkey without bumping a mountain. In spite of its twists and turns the single track railway spanning the wild territory was unable to escape the inevitable and by midday we were in the awesome grip of a million-year-old result of a volcanic convulsion. Through enormous clefts in the rock barriers we crawled following the usual flooded river which had learnt the easiest route long before the railway. Hissing imposingly, its pistons pounding, the big locomotive dragged its cargo at a walking pace up the severe incline. Given the slightest encouragement it stopped at the smallest of stations to allow northbound trains to pass. There would follow a frantic competition between thirsty locomotive and soot-covered passengers to take on water, the source frequently being one and the same. Vendors of food disembarked at every halt to make room for others with replenished stocks who boarded the train.

Food plays a vital part in a Turkish railway journey. In spite of a continuous cavalcade of vendors shouting their wares up and down the corridors every traveller carries vast stocks with him. To my amazement most of the bundles and boxes belonging to my Syrian and Turkish travelling companions contained loaves of bread, fruit, home-made cakes, joints of cooked meat and various bottles of liquid refreshment. Hardly an hour out of Hayderpasa and I was pressed to join the melee as Turk and Syrian pooled their resources and made swift inroads into them. As there was a restaurant car attached to the train I had purchased no more than the odd snack so my own contribution was nothing more than a couple of bars of chocolate and some Bulgarian cheese. But I was solemnly warned off the restaurant car. It's dirty, they said. I could well believe it!

Occasionally our rations were supplemented by delicacies from the vendors. These ranged from kebab, the roasting of which was carried out on the spot in little portable home-made charcoal burners, to a kind of Turkish delight and a sweet-meat that looked like cotton wool. Bargaining was surprisingly infrequent though my companions saw to it that in my few dealings with vendors I was not overcharged. One visitor into the compartment was a youth intent upon imparting the word of God. I suppose I looked a likely convert for he loosed onto me an unending torrent from the Scriptures (or maybe the Koran). I nodded knowingly not wishing to hurt the man's feelings until my Syrians gleefully imparted the news that I was unable to understand a word he was saying!

The most un-Turkish city in Turkey is its capital. True, I only saw a bit of Ankara and at night but for the couple of hours I was able to wonder in Ataturk boulevard and Kizilay Square I might have been in Birmingham or Milan. The citadel and the old town in the north were hidden by the night and an old woman in the baggy trousers of her country cousins drew stares as she waddled past the fashionable shops.

I arrived back at the station to discover that we had an uninvited guest in the compartment. He hadn't *come in* I was told; he had *fallen in*. Drunk as the proverbial lord my Syrian friends had propped him up in a corner seat, retrieved his spectacles and pipe, and dusted him down. Promptly he rolled full-length on the seat and, finding this to his liking, settled down for the night. Indignant at what we thought might be a ruse to obtain a whole length of seat to himself we pushed him back into his corner from whence the whole performance was repeated. How long this would have gone on had the contingencies of nature not taken a hand it was impossible to say. Suddenly he sat up and asked for the bathroom. We told him that this was not a royal train. "Train," he mumbled through his big drooping moustache as if he had never heard of such a phenomenon. "What train?" We pushed him out into the corridor then drew the blinds and barricaded the door against his return. By this time Ankara was miles away. The poor devil was going to get a horrible shock to go with his hangover in the morning. We never saw him again.

Morning brought a stupendous sight. Looking out of the window and risking the showers of smuts I saw the railway making a bee-line across the flat Anatolian plain straight for the enormous bulk of the Taurus Mountains. The dawn sun splashed the vivid whiteness of the peaks dazzling the eye and reflecting upon the wisps of cloud that hung to their summits.

For the next seven hours halts were numerous, both scheduled and unscheduled. The stations were simply clearings where a double track could be laid to allow for trains to pass. Life for the few inhabitants revolved around the arrival and departure of trains and children ran amok amongst the shunting wagons.

Great blobs of pink and white blossom softened the sombre background of wild mountain scenery but as we climbed towards the snow-line this gradually gave way to barren rock. Herds of goats and, incongruously, the odd camel, were the only living things in the desolate region while, above, soared an occasional eagle. The train crept at less than a walking pace for mile after mile through ravine and chasm and almost was there an air of festivity at the little summit station as if in perpetual celebration of the negotiation of the worst perils of the journey.

From there onwards the locomotive became a hound unleased. It pounded down the inclines, hissing and snorting, rushing through a series of tunnels, filling everything with acrid smoke and whistling joyfully. Already two hours behind schedule it not unnaturally was frequently held up by signals. This was an excuse for the most ear-splitting crescendo of whistles it has ever been my misfortune to hear. The mountains threw the echoes back and the longer the signal remained at red the more prolonged was the banshee howl rising to a furious unearthly screech. I marvelled that such sound existed and at the fact that enough steam remained to drive the pistons when an unfortunate signalman, driven half-insane by the noise, allowed, in desperation, the train to pass.

The peace of the Cilician Plain made almost as much contrast as that of the fickle weather. Cold and showery in the mountains it was suddenly hot and humid. I watched the distant mountains revert to their picture-postcard remoteness as we ground into Adana three hours late, a state of affairs that worried nobody. I made the round of farewells and descended from a train that had become a home.

For the fourth largest town in Turkey Adana was a disappointment. Most of the buildings were mud brick with here and there a square concrete edifice by which status it ranked as a city. Never have I seen a place so overloaded with banks, yet only one would accept a travel cheque—and even then casting some doubt on the validity of Messrs Barclay.

My hotel was full of surprises. A shower that actually produced hot water even if it did flood most of the first floor, a lift that had to be coaxed upwards by play on the buttons like the operation of an accordion, and a maid who wanted my autograph. My bedroom was reasonably clean even if the whiteness of the bedsheets would have rated the "other detergent" in a TV commercial.

The guide book spoke of Adana as being a city afflicted by frequent thunderstorms in summer. It wasn't summer but the affliction remained. I was halfway to the air terminus when it struck. Within minutes the wide streets of Adana were raging torrents of muddy water.

It continued raining hard well into the night and bed seemed the place to be, particularly since sleep had become a rarity on this journey. Accordingly I dined at the nearest restaurant on fish hash—a kind of Turkish *bouillabaisse*—and was between the off-white sheets in my hotel by eight.

Though a stifling sun tried to make amends Adana was a bedraggled sight next morning. Squelching through the mud I made the air terminus and I was the only passenger on the dilapidated coach that deposited me at the airport. The flight from Adana to Beirut was a twice weekly affair and seemingly quite an event. A large crowd had gathered to watch the arrival—an hour late—from Ankara of the Vanguard of Turkish Airlines and the chaos that existed in the customs and immigration lounges had a distinct flavour of Victoria Station. When at last we were able to make our way to the aircraft everything had to be held up another few minutes while two heavily robed moslems took it into their heads to unroll their prayer rugs, fling themselves down on the concrete tarmac and effect their devotions.

The flight was little more than an hour. Over the left wing the miniature sky-scrapers of Beirut appeared at the head of a choppy white-flecked sea. We came in low over the south-western suburbs and landed at the big international airport. "Welcome to Lebanon," said the signs. That we had arrived in a country virtually at war was made abundantly clear the moment we stepped from the aircraft. Armed soldiers stood around in bunches waiting for something to happen and the welcome to Lebanon deteriorated into long and frustrating hold-ups at the passport desk and customs bay. Tired though I was I found myself at that moment looking forward to the return journey. The bit in between, I thought, was going to be a bit of a bore.

I was wrong of course. Though it had lost its Victorian elegance the journey had been so full of events, interest and the mosaic of strange lands, new customs and big-hearted people that a sojourn in one place smacked of an anti-climax. To many the route to a far destination, whether it be one for business or pleasure, is just distance to be covered by the fastest and easiest method possible. "Fly and win yourself an extra day's holiday", shout the travel brochures completely overlooking the fascination that lies hidden beneath the air routes.

For me the journey had been the reason for my visit to Beirut. And that surely is how it should be.